Socialising the Antisocial Bank

Converting the antisocial bank by digitally connecting with customers to become part of their community

Book 2 of The Complete Banker series

By Chris Skinner

The
Complete Banker

First published 2010 by Balatro Limited, 98 Westbury Lane, Buckhursthill, IG9 5PW, UK

ISBN 978-1-907720-07-9

Edited and produced by Searching Finance Ltd, 8 Whitehall Road, London W7 2JE, UK. Tel: +44 (0) 7885 441682; email: enquiries@searchingfinance.co.uk; web: www.searchingfinance.co.uk

Editor: Mabel Wale

Typeset by: Deirdré Gyenes

Socialising the Antisocial Bank

Converting the antisocial bank by digitally connecting with customers to become part of their community

Book 2 of The Complete Banker series

By Chris Skinner

The
Complete Banker

About Chris Skinner

Chris has been providing independent, expert commentary on the key developments in banking for over a decade in his role as Chief Executive of Balatro and Chairman of the Financial Services Club. In particular, he has been writing for various media, such as *The Banker* Magazine, since 2004 and is a key commentator on banking for prime time news channels including the BBC, Sky and Bloomberg. Prior to creating his independent entities, Chris had key roles at management and board levels covering insurance, retail and investment banking across a range of consulting and technology firms.

Chris Skinner has worked worldwide delivering advice, keynote speeches, presentations and workshops to many banks and vendors worldwide, including Accenture, American Express, ANZ, Bank of America, Bank of Baroda, Cisco, Hewlett Packard, Liberty Bank, Lloyds TSB, McKinsey, Merrill Lynch, Microsoft, National Australia Bank, Nationwide Building Society, NCR, TATA, the National Bank of Kuwait, the Union Bank of the Philippines, Wachovia Bank, Washington Mutual, and many others.

About the Financial Services Club

The Financial Services Club is a unique service aimed at senior executives and decision makers from banks, insurance companies, technology firms, consultancies ... in fact, any firm that is interested in understanding and planning for the future operating environment for the financial services markets.

The Financial Services Club bridges the gap between today and tomorrow. It allows you to network with hundreds of professionals all sharing a common interest in the future of the industry. The Club hosts over 50 events a year, in a number of different European countries, with keynote speakers and luminaries from the industry airing their views on the future of financial services. Our illustrious speaker list is targeted to cover all aspects of the industry from practitioners to legislators to futurists.

For more information, go to http://www.fsclub.co.uk

Contents

Chapter 2 Social media's challenges

Chapter 3 Twitter, Facebook and other social networks

Chapter 4 Social finance

Chapter 5 Social money and virtual worlds

Chapter 6 Social media in practice

Preface

I had thought about calling this book 'The Social Bank', but that's pretty meaningless as most banks are anti-social. They do not engage with customers to 'delight' or 'exceed their expectations', and the majority are happy to receive a C-minus for service. Why is this?

Mainly because customers cannot find a better deal elsewhere or, if they can, they cannot be bothered. In other words we mistake loyalty in banking for what is actually customer inertia.

But why are customers so lackadaisical? Because banks are pretty much a homogeneous group. In fact, some might suggest there is no competition in banking when hardly any new entrants can be seen and this is down to the fact that banking is highly regulated, and the regulations creat major barriers to entry.

That does not mean it cannot change.

For example, social lending services are growing. Zopa, the first of such services, has now enabled over £100 million ($150 million) to be lent and borrowed between its users since launch in 2005 through 2010. That's small beans compared to bank lending, but their portfolio is doubling year on year.

Similarly, social currencies are growing fast, with almost $5 billion traded in social gaming units online in 2009.

And being social 24*7 via Facebook and Twitter on your Android or iPhone means that the social revolution is rapidly turning this planet on its head.

After all, who would have thought that a social world of 500 million people would gather in one place by 2010? That place is Facebook.

So, if you want to work out how to be a social bank and connect with your targeted communities of customers, this is a short guide as to how to do it.

Meantime, if you want to become a complete banker, then keep adding our small works of observations about the industry to your knowledge by buying some of the other books about banking in the Complete Banker series.

Have fun and enjoy the read,

Chris

PS: The articles herein have been selected from white papers, presentations and other research I have undertaken, and from my regular Financial Services Club blog postings at http://www.thefinanser.com; for more information on the Financial Services Club, go to http://www.fsclub.co.uk

Chapter 1 The future of banking is social

Introduction

In the mid-2000s, a revolution took place on the internet, with mobile internet and easy-to-use tools changing the game. Referred to by many as Web 2.0, I prefer to talk about this as the social web. It basically means that the world has moved from a network of people consuming information, to a network of people sharing news about their lives. These social tools range from Facebook to Twitter, and from YouTube to Flickr. Banks have done a good job of ignoring this revolution, but they do so at their peril, as social finance is going to change the basics of banking fundamentally in the long term.

Social media in finance – survey points to the future (2010)

Brett King, author of the new book Bank 2.0 (published by Marshall Cavendish, 2010), which I can recommend to those of you working with social media in finance as a focus, has worked with me in analysing the initial and general results from the Financial Services Club social media survey.

Almost 450 folks responded to the survey; here are a few fast facts:

- The majority of the participants would participate in social media before making a decision on a financial service provider;
- 93 per cent of participants consider social networking will be worthwhile or critical for banks in the next five years;
- 78 per cent said social media is worthwhile or critical for corporate banking relationships today;
- The majority of customers would go first to independent community discussions before coming to the brand itself;
- Facebook and Twitter scored as the highest value social media channels for retail banking engagements;

- LinkedIn, blogs and privately managed online communities scored as the highest value social media channels for business interactions;
- 74 per cent said their use of social media organisationally will increase over the next two years, while only 1 per cent said it would decrease.

Our conclusions

93 per cent of the 443 respondents indicated that a focus on social media would be essential to the future of financial institutions over the next five years. Only 1 per cent of the survey group said that they felt their organisation would be likely to decrease their use of social media in the next two years ... only 1 per cent! All indications are that this is a hot topic for pretty much every service organisation out there, which is surprising as so few firms are doing anything about it!

Adoption rate of social media is scary. Two years ago Twitter was unheard of. Although Twitter started beta testing their concept in 2006, it is largely agreed that it didn't formally launch till April 2007. Since then Twitter has taken off by storm – globally, in the US and in Australia, Twitter ranks as the 12th most popular website by traffic, in the UK it ranks in the top 10, and in most of the EU it ranks in the top 30 or 50 websites. It took Facebook four years to achieve the same impact; so social media adoption is definitely speeding up, not slowing down.

Given the rate at which Facebook, Twitter and other such social networking sites have impacted popular culture, it should come as no surprise that financial service providers are starting to think about integrating social media into their business. However, the path to integration of these new media tools into the institution is a tough challenge. Firstly, organisations understand that this is an issue requiring total commitment across the organisation, but achieving such is difficult because finding someone who can garner that support is a challenge. Secondly, brands in general are starting to understand that social media is a medium they can't 'spin' – that is, customers are largely in control – and that is worrying, particularly in the current environment where financial institutions are facing significant perception challenges at large.

The real conclusions of our research show that, individually, we know that it is inevitable that social media will be integrated into our business, but our organisations are looking for direction. The difficulty is that there is no 'one size fits all' solution. Each of the popular social networking sites works in different ways, so we need strategies that reflect this. The survey showed, for example, that LinkedIn is a far better tool for business-to-business discussions and for promotion of services to professional individuals, such as priority banking and wealth management. For general brand marketing, Facebook is an effective tool, but our respondents wouldn't use Facebook for banking contacts or LinkedIn for private and personal socialising. So banks must target effectively if they are to get the socialisation of finance right. The strategy needs to be localised and involves pay-per-click embedded advertising as well as sponsored groups and consumer support.

Twitter as a tool is an excellent research tool. We would say that this medium in its current form would probably provide more data than your best-of-breed focus groups and customer satisfaction surveys if it can be harnessed correctly. When it comes to Twitter, it is all about listening. Our survey showed that consumers would use social media first to ask other customers about their experience with your brand, rather than engaging with your brand directly.

The survey shows the biggest missed opportunities for banks and financial service providers are more in respect to their own properties. Banks need to be using blogs to give more of their own voice to the social discussions, along with privately owned social networks embedded into the customer website experience. If you are not sure what privately owned social networks mean, think, say, Amazon's product recommendations and rating system, PayPal's Blog, and Wells Fargo's Stagecoach Island?

Our survey essentially shows that most banks are missing a key development in customer engagement – both at the consumer and, more importantly, at the corporate level – by not deploying and utilising this media effectively. For example, respondents are familiar with some of the key bank-provided B2B networks, such as those from Bank of America and HSBC, but these examples are few and far between. This is the case even though most consumers and corporations feel this is critical to the future!

There needs to be an immediate and concerted effort to integrate social media into your organisation today. More than that, this needs to be a cross-discipline, multi-department effort and it's going to be difficult, but not necessarily expensive. If used properly, the bank will improve delivery, revenue and customer engagement significantly.

Banks ignore social media at their peril (2009)

There is a view that banks are only just getting to grips with the net and learning about mobile, and see no point in the social media space at all. But I completely disagree. Social media and networks, social banking and social money should be a major focus for banks. Let's look at these areas and their relevance to banks and banking in more depth.

First of all, let's define our terms.

Social media is like mainstream media but user-generated. It's blogging instead of newspapers; YouTube instead of TV; and podcasting instead of radio. It's media, but social media. Social networking is like real-world networking but online.

So it's Facebook, MySpace, Bebo, QQ, Badoo and more. It's where people date, talk, meet, relate and even work together, on occasion. It's networking, but socially and remotely.

Social banking is providing bank services but, in a similar fashion, through social methods. It is the process of personalising banking and enabling people and businesses to see the people and businesses they are saving and investing with. It's Zopa and Prosper, Wesabe and Mint, and many more.

Social money is the way to make payments peer-to-peer, and has already taken off big time with PayPal, but now has many other pretenders, especially in the mobile space.

On that last point, please note that all of these services are based upon Internet Protocols (IP) as the platform, but may be delivered through any device including TV, PC, mobile and Blackberry.

As mentioned, social media replaces traditional media as a source of news, views and entertainment. Already, most TV is being watched online. This does not mean that the TV has been replaced by the internet as the primary entertainment source but, for a large range of demographics, this may be the case.

Meanwhile, how many of you pick up a paper every morning to read? How many of you pick up a free newspaper these days? It's free because print news is worthless. It's out-of-date by the time it hits the streets, so you read it more for the tactile feel, the fact you don't have access to the net or TV, and for the opinions and commentary.

When working at the home office, my usual office, then my morning is typically made up of reading a number of daily alerts from news sources, including traditional ones such as the *Financial Times,* and reading them online. Many of these alerts are from blogs, diggs and other sources, however. So it's social. I read what the crowd I follow read. If my mates say a story is worthy, then it's worth reading. That's social.

Finally, I only really listen to the radio when in the car. Otherwise, if I'm on the train or in the gym I'm listening to podcasts. Downloaded radio podcasts, as well as news and views from industry punters and individuals.

This is the world of social media.

So how can a bank make money out of social media?

Bear in mind, I'm not talking here about social networking, banking or money, just media. To be honest, I don't think a bank should try to make money out of social media. Social media is not there for money-making but for customer engagement, which leads to money-making.

And what does it mean for customer engagement? Well, on the one hand, it's understanding customer attitudes and ideas. If customers are out there saying the bank is awful, horrible, difficult, complacent, arrogant, greedy or worse, then it's engaging with those customers to find out why they think the bank is all of those things.

It's more than counteracting negative views, though; it's looking for ways to engage with people to create positive experiences. Start posting stories that help those people out there who are struggling with finance, for example, by proactively advising them. This tends to be the domain of independent blogs and aggregator sites today, although there are some great bank examples in this space, such as Royal Bank of Canada's site aimed at students.

What these sites do is create a relationship with people, through news, views, advice and ideas. That's the point of social media: to create a conversation that leads to a relationship that leads to trust that, eventually, leads to business.

So there is a point to this after all, and banks can make money out of social media.

Not social networking, banking or money, social media. Money out of blogging, podcasting and posting videos on YouTube. (...)

Banks don't get social media. Many are trying, but they're not there yet. Banks don't get the world of social media or social networking, and certainly have not even tapped into the potential of social banking.

This is a huge mistake, however, as, it's too easy to dismiss because it just appears to be a boondoggle

If that were the case, then how come most of my relationships are accessible through my mobile and online channels? How come most of my influencers come through those channels? How come mainstream media means nothing anymore, as I'm using social media to determine most of my thoughts, actions, ideas and investments?

Let me say that again: "I'm using social media to determine most of my thoughts, actions, ideas and investments".

It does not mean that I've dropped mainstream media entirely, but it's integrated with my social media and the two balance each other to determine who I trust and invest with.

That's the point. The point is that social media creates a conversation that leads to relationships that leads to trust that leads to business.

Ignore this space at your future peril.

Social media's relevance to banks (2009)

Let's look at the relevance of social media to banks.

The usual question I get from banks is: 'Does it make money?' Sure, for Mark Zuckenberg and Biz Stone, the founders of Facebook and Twitter respectively, of course it will make money ... but for the rest of us?

The problem for banks is that asking whether social media will make money is the wrong question. The question should be: 'What is the relevance of social media to banks?'

You see, the former question assumes you are getting into this to make money and the answer is, you don't make any money directly out of social media. This is because social media is social. It's there to have a conversation: to debate, discourse and discuss. It is not a platform for directly making money.

But then, neither is marketing or sponsorship or corporate hospitality or any form of promotional investment ... not directly, anyways. That doesn't mean that you stop marketing, sponsoring, entertaining or promoting though, does it?

And there's the core point: social media is exactly that. It is media. Another form of communications channel alongside television, radio, newsprint and related media. The point of this media, however, is that it is far more entertaining and inclusive than any other form of media because it is interactive, two-way conversations, rather than just one-way broadcasts. So, for those of you who aren't Facebooking or Twittering yet, here's why it is relevant to banks.

Imagine you are running a bank advertisement and your customer(s) could tell you what they think about it.

Imagine you are launching a new account with a superb interest rate, and your customers could tell you what your competition is doing.

Imagine you are considering opening a branch in Tumbleweed and the residents of Tumbleweed could tell you whether they want one before you invest a cent ... instantaneously and in real time.

Finally, imagine you go to the expense of opening a branch in Tumbleweed after extensive research, and a significant budget deployed for planning, developing, building and marketing the new branch ... only to find that the real audience you should be serving are in neighbouring Cyberville and it would have cost you hardly a bean to launch there.

It's this last point that is the most critical point for banks to understand today.

If you are still working in a 20th century world of 'branch distribution' in a 'multi-channel mix' using 'integrated media campaigns' supported by a strong percentage of 'online marketing' ... you are dead meat.

We no longer have multi-channels and online ... we just have real time. Real-time experiences across multiple points of contact. And if you think in that 21st century way – it's all about real-time experiences – then you can start to see the relevance of social media.

And the real relevance is that:

- Two out of three people on the planet visit social networks (Nielsen, 2009);
- Visiting social sites is now the fourth most popular online activity – ahead of personal email – 66.8% of Internet users have used social networks, while only 65.1% have used email (Nielsen, 2009);
- Social media is democratising communications, with over a million blog posts written every day by people like you and me;
- YouTube has over 100 million viewers worldwide;
- 13 hours of video is uploaded to YouTube every minute;
- 100 million YouTube videos are watched every day;
- 13 million articles are now stored on Wikipedia;
- 3.6 billion photos are archived on Flickr (June 2009);
- 93% of social media users believe a company should have a presence in social media (Cone, 2008);
- 85% of social media users believe that a company should go further than just having a presence on social sites and should also interact with its customers (Cone, 2008).

These numbers scream one conclusion: if a bank is not actively engaged in social media and using it to dialogue with their customers, it is the equivalent of a bank seeing all of their customers moving out of Tumbleweed to live in Cyberville and saying: "Oh, we like it here. We're not moving."

As a long-term strategy, a bank that lives in a place with no people is not a good thing.

In summary, if you really want to know what the relevance of social media is to banks, then take a note of this quote from *Business Week* in February 2009:

"For companies, resistance to social media is futile. Millions of people are creating content for the social web. Your competitors are already there. Your customers have been there for a long time. If your business isn't putting itself out there, it ought to be."

The transformational power of social media (2010)

There are a number of technologies that we see as key to addressing the regulatory and innovatory requirements of the 2010s.

One of these is social media, which plays a critical role in all aspects of society and banking.

(...)

In the last five years there has been a revolution in communications via technology. The social revolution. This social revolution is reflected in key developments demonstrated by the massive societal move to use Facebook, and its localised equivalents. Facebook has over 400 million users. It is the largest communication, entertainment, news and discussion channel on the planet. It has more influence with more people than their teachers, bankers, politicians and business leaders.

That's transformational.

Alongside the march of Facebook has been the correlated developments of Twitter. Viewed by many as a transient phenomena, the reason why Twitter hit the news is that it provides the news, in real-time. The typical users of Twitter are actually over 35 years of age, and they use it to keep up with the BBC, Al-Jazeera, CNN and other news services, as well as the most influential voices in their business and social communities. The fact that Twitter allowed the world to be informed of the Haitian earthquake, the G20 protests and the Iranian revolts in real time demonstrated the power of connections to any individual on the planet in real-time globally.

That's transformational.

In looking at such transformations, we have to ask: what is your bank doing to exploit these opportunities?

Social networks don't need banks, they need friends (2009)

Social networks have been on the rise for a while and I define them as places where people gather digitally to share a common interest. That's not the classical definition by the way, such as these from Wikipedia:

> "A social network is a social structure made of nodes (which are generally individuals or organizations) that are tied by one or more specific types of interdependency, such as values, visions, ideas, financial exchange, friendship, kinship, dislike, conflict or trade.
>
> "A social network service focuses on building online communities of people who share interests and activities, or who are interested in exploring the interests and activities of others."

So we all now know what these are, and there are many examples from Facebook to Club Penguin and from Bebo to MySpace.

What you may not know is that the number of people using these sites today number over 600 million individuals, according to Comscore. That's one in 10 people on the planet, and one in three internet users.

The number of users is still rising at 25 per cent per annum average, with the Middle East and Africa being the fastest rising community, but this is a worldwide phenomena. For example, 85 per cent of Brazilian and Canadian internet users participate in social networks online, compared with 78 per cent of Brits and 70 per cent of Americans.

That's a lot of people. Why are they all flocking to social networks? Because it's life augmentation.

These days folks talk about 'life streams' and that's what it's all about – sharing your life with friends who are local and remote. Sharing your life is all about your emotions, activities, sports and hobbies, photos and videos, anything really. And the people sharing their lives are not all youths, which is the common assumption, as the average social network user is a woman of 39 with children, who is sharing her family's life with friends and extended family. Equally, one of the fastest rising groups is older people, not young folks. So that blows quite a few myths away for a start.

It's not all about Facebook either. Facebook is the largest of the networks in the English speaking world, now beating MySpace into first place, but don't ignore local language sites such as Sonico in Latin America or QQ in China.

It's also not a new phenomena. Friendster and Friends Reunited have been around for a long time before these networks but, like blogging, the new generation of social network is just much easier to use.

Anyways, my aim here is not to define this market. You can find that sort of stuff anywhere. It's to talk about the relevance of these developments to banks.

What I find interesting in this context is that most banks ban the use of social networks at work. The result was, until this became mainstream, that I spent most of my time trying to explain what the hell a social network was. I hope I don't have to do that today, but still find some bankers struggle with why this stuff works.

It is also worth pointing out that it is only since June 2008 that I've found bankers generally who are familiar with what this is ... that's about three years after this became noted by most industries and about a year after most industries rolled out new business services to tap into these markets.

Ah well, what the hell has a social network got to do with banking anyway?

Quite a lot, actually. Social media educates, advises and supports, which builds relationships and trust. So do social networks.

These days I might throw out the question to friends and family via Facebook, "does anyone know which bank we can trust these days?" Try it and see what happens ... mind you, if you're a banker reading this, you may not want to try that particular question. With banks no longer trusted thanks to the credit crisis, and demise of WaMu and Northern Rock and more, people are wondering who to trust.

Who ya gonna trust?

Bankbusters! And who are bankbusters? Your friends and family. That is why social networks are critical to banks to gain future business, as recommenders will come through your network and their influence will be immense.

So how can a bank influence the influencers? Advertising? No. Investing in building their own social networks? Not really ... although there are a few who have, such as Fortis, Bank of America and HSBC.

These efforts are all tapping into the small business markets, where managers and entrepreneurs with small and growing businesses need as much support and advice as they can get. That is what these banks have established as platforms to support and advise them.

Fortis began this process with Join2Grow, a brilliant effort with zero overt advertising for the bank. Bank of America followed with their small business community, and HSBC recently launched the HSBC Business Network.

The aim of these services is to create increased loyalty and revenue by assisting the smaller business community with advice and support. That makes sense and is a good entrée for any bank to get into this field.

As we move into Facebook, banks are also doing some other interesting things, such as the Bank of America's Medal Me application and H&R Block who are doing lots of stuff in Facebook from funky videos in a youth style to tax applications that are fun!

Apart from these experiments however, I have yet to see banks make much out of social networks, but then I've yet to see anyone make much out of social networks in a financial context (apart from the people who created them).

These networks are not for finance, you see. They are for advice and support.

This is why the only things financially related that you notice in Facebook are applications such as Pay Me, Spare Change and PayPal. This is because these are methods to pay between friends, and friends are what you focus upon in social networks, not banking.

So I guess that's my conclusion in general.

From a purely social networking viewpoint, banks need to focus upon methods they can use to become friends with their participants in their networks. Friends advise and support, they don't sell, charge and make money out of you. By advising and supporting, banks can build relationships and trust and so, like social media, it will result in advocacy from your 'fans' who then became loyal and easier to do business with.

That is the point: building trust and loyalty.

What exactly have banks done so far to make good use of social media? (2008)

ING, ABN AMRO, Royal Bank of Scotland, Saxo Bank, BNP Paribas, Deutsche Bank and a few others have messed about with Second Life. Similarly, TD Waterhouse, Royal Bank of Canada, JPMorgan, the Co-operative Bank, Bank of America and a few others have thrashed around with social network experiments. A few have tried to make a really strategic deployment to leverage this space, such as Wells Fargo, who have spent serious dollars on virtual worlds and blogs; and Fortis with the Join2Grow website, which is a real innovation for small business networking online. Bank of America's copy for small business isn't bad, but Fortis has created a site that doesn't even carry its brand, which is why they get the reward. Social networks are not for branding, as people shun this in the real world, they are to provide platforms of participation. That's what Fortis and Wells Fargo have been trying to create.

Regardless of whether what these banks are doing is good or bad, at least they are all trying and I'm sure some are reaping benefits.

The 'World of Me' (2010)

(...)

Everything today is mashable. I can mix and match pieces of functionality from all over the mobile internet into a lifestyle structure that suits the World of Me. This has fundamentally changed things because I can now design the World of Me. The World of Me is defined by how I structure and connect with friends, companies, governments, media and more. It defines how I structure and connect with everything, including and especially for banks and banking. For media, the World of Me is defined by the blogs I consume, the YouTube videos I watch, the diggs and RSS feeds I absorb, the tweets I read ... I create my world, which is why iPhone, iPad and iPod.

I is everything. Me is all. It sounds very selfish but it's not. It's actually about me designing the world around me. That is the world we, and especially me, lives in. I want to publish my thoughts – I can. I want this in print on Amazon – simple. I want to share my music – no worries.

I want to get my bank to work around me ...

Hmmmm. Bit more difficult, that one.

Sure, you could use social credits or Hyve payments, but they all need to be backed by a banking system that has not changed much in the last decade.

For example, how do I interact with my bank? Via a dull online bank statement that looks just like my old printed bank statement? Via a call centre and branch, with these interactions appearing to have no relationship with the online or mobile bank, and no ability to access these services via my net-based banking service? Via a bank that has no blog, no social interactions electronically and, only if I'm very lucky indeed, might respond to an email to open an account?

This will change, of course, as new entrants open up new social finance services and a few innovative banks interact electronically via tweets and status updates.

But what will really revolutionise this world is when a bank offers all of their services as individual apps, gadgets, widgets and wikis, to plug and play into the World of Me and my internet lifestyle.

This is a theme I have regularly explored, and continue to play with today.

When I can design my bank services around me, by taking a little bit of transaction servicing from bank A's widget, a snippet of card services via bank B's app, and a sprinkle of P2P payments via bank C's wiki, then I'll truly be living in a world of 21st century banking.

Oh shoot – this is the 21st century!

Why has social media been so successful? (2009)

It's about relationship and connections.

People get technology today not because it's gadgets but because it is connecting their lives to the lives of countless friends and strangers.

This is why Facebook can go from nothing to a place with the population of the US in under four years, and why Twitter can go from off-the-radar to on-everyone's-radar in just under a year.

Last year, no-one mentioned Twitter. Today, it's an integral part of the show. But it's only integral because it helps people manage, share and organise their lives and loves.

And that's what banks have to do if they are to reconnect. They must connect people to their money and finances in a simple and easy way.

Everyone keeps referring to the Facebook and Twitter generation, or the 'twitfaced' generation as some might call them. Who are the twitfaced generation? They're not the under-25s. They're not the under-35s. They are the over-35s. Most Facebook and Twitter users are average age of 40. So when we talk about social networks, we are not talking about the next generation of customers. We are talking about the current generation.

So what we're really saying is that you need to completely rethink the bank around social technologies and rethink the branch network by closing most of it down and reinvesting that saving into social finance.

If you don't, you're dead. Give it less than a decade, and you're dead. I'm serious.

Mainstream media fought this battle ... and lost. That's why television and newspapers are shutting down by the bucket load as today's media is created by me on YouTube and Typepad.

So stop fighting the lost bank cause of the branch network.

Rethink it.

How to break trust with social media (2009)

I was going to post a bunch of stuff about our Financial Services Club meeting discussing how banks could use social networks and social media, but then saw that Karl Flinders, a guest of the Club, beat me to it. Writing for *Computer Weekly*, Karl posted a nice little note entitled: 'The truth about banks, Facebook and Twitter'.

Obviously listening attentively to our panel, he captured a few golden quotes and nuggets such as:

- "If you want to adopt social media you need to listen to what people are saying";
- "Banks will have to get used to the idea that there will be some customers who will want to use the web";
- "In financial services we are still in the educational phase";

- "There will be a bonus for banks that experiment early with social media";
- "Social media is a good way of engaging with employees as well as customer."

The significance of social media has been demonstrated by the Iranain elections, G20 protests and more, and their use of Twitter to share news and knowledge globally. Without Twitter, these people would be unable to share their message and have anyone even remotely aware of what was happening on the streets, as it can be vetted by news agencies (both Iranian and British).

That is why I am interested in Twitter and social media, as it gives me raw information to make up my own mind about the truth as well as a new channel of communication.

It is also why I recommend that banks focus upon Twitter, YouTube, Facebook, Flickr and other tools of this nature, as they offer a low cost with broad reach communication channel. A channel that can reach 200 million people or more at no cost.

These channels are there to create trust and have a conversation. That's why they are social. They are not there for a hard sell of products and advertising. Otherwise, they would be called commercial.

That's why there is so much confusion about how to use these social channels to create commerce.

The answer is: talk and listen, engage and dialogue, converse and socialise ... then, if the folks you are conversing with want to, they will click through to your commercial sites because they trust you won't stitch them up.

But don't try to achieve the latter first – the commercial sale that is, not the stitch-up! You only get to the sale by getting people to participate in your community, your social network, your circle of trust.

And whatever you do, don't break the trust of the social network.

A sense of community (2007)

I find it interesting that we have very few social network examples to point at in banking.

Zopa is often referred to as a great financial social network, but it's not a bank. After Zopa and it's followers such as Prosper, I struggle to think of many other banking social networks.

And yet it's strange because social networking is all about having a sense of community, a feeling of belonging to that community, a passion for sharing with that community and a relationship with that community.

The reason this is strange is that yesterday I flew to the US and today I'm sleepless in Seattle. It's three in the morning and my jet lag is keeping me on the night lane. I'm here to present to a group of community banks on how to deal with the internet age. The challenges of Web 2.0 and the issues therein.

So I wrote that paragraph above, about social networking being all about community, and then thought about the fact that these banks are called community banks. There is a connection there ... it's called community.

Whatever we say about new technologies, the internet age and all this stuff, the fact that email, instant messaging, SMS texts, mobile telephones, Facebook poking and all this stuff works is because it's about community.

Communications create community.

Both stem from the Latin meaning of commune, which means to 'give amongst each other'. To share. To belong. In other words, it's all about human relationships.

Maybe that is what some banks have lost sight of during the past decades of cost-cutting automation, but it's something they'll have to think carefully around if they are to survive in the internet age.

Why are (UK) banks ignoring new media? (2009)

Recent UK bank TV advertising (e.g. NatWest) as focused on its trusted relationship with the customer, through its professed virtues of providing good, honest advice in troubled times. Sounds great in principle but, in practice, something has fundamentally changed. The confidence has gone. The trust is blemished. The bank's brand is not the same.

Wrapped up in the folds of the Royal Bank of Scotland and Sir Fred Goodwin daily headlines, the idea of giving good money sense advice is a bit laughable.

This is not to say that NatWest and other banks shouldn't advertise but, as I will discuss later, they should stop spending on advertising in traditional media only and start leveraging new media.

Customers are more aware of their finances than ever and do not trust institutions that have bad headlines, bad rates or bad vibes. That's why folks are churning their money around, looking as far as they can for a flight to safety.

For example, I've already said a few times that some of the less flashy banks are doing quite well, as are some of the mutual institutions such as the Nationwide Building Society. Nationwide do advertise, but their focus is much more around being lovable, nice and working in the customer's interests because you are a member of the Nationwide, not a customer.

And all of this is focused around branch-based banking debates. In branches, the idea of money sense and rewards programs for staying with the bank probably seem great in the marketing corridors of head offices but, in the high road, far more convincing is the human experience of staff you trust and like, and brands you see as being trusted and liked.

Result? Nationwide's new account openings have risen massively in the last year.

Banks with branches fighting for trust and confidence could learn something from the consumer championing, member-based interest approaches of the building society sector as a whole, not just the Nationwide.

The real point is that those who want to be able to touch their financier's bricks and mortar may well find that the prudent and quiet thrifts gain a 'trusted' position over those who feature in the headlines every day as being the creators of the financial crisis.

So what should the banks with damaged brands do? Stop advertising in mainstream media.

Funnily enough, Nielsen came out with some analysis of this area, and the headline was: 'Banks should advertise more to regain consumer confidence'.

The Financial Brand picks through the meat of this news though and, like me, concludes that banks should stop advertising on TV if their brand is damaged. So what should they do? Focus upon leveraging remote relationships through new media.

The fact is that UK banks are mainly fighting a branch-based battle and totally ignoring online and remote channels. UK banks' ideas of marketing online are, to be honest, pathetic. Oh, a banner ad here, a link placement there. Great. Doesn't work though.

Where are NatWest's online or viral campaigns? Where's its blog? Where's HBOS, Lloyds, Barclays or Nationwide blogs for that matter? They don't exist or, if they do, then they're very well hidden as I can't find them and I'm looking. Google these company names and the word 'blog', and nothing official comes back.

The fact is that the only UK banks I've noticed doing anything with Facebook, MySpace, Twitter or new media is the Co-operative Bank, which created a few nice green pages on MySpace two years ago (note this attempt to network has now been deleted); Barclaycard, whose advert for contactless gained great viral viewing; and Lloyds TSB, whose irritating theme tune made the charts.

Mind you, rather than their annoying advert tune, you are far more likely to find a YouTube customer-generated advert such as 'I fought the Lloyds and the Lloyds lost' instead of a bank-generated ad, when looking for some form of online presence.

So here's the rub.

Banks today are stuck in branches fighting for customer confidence through traditional marketing media where they position themselves as trusted. Meanwhile, customers are searching online for advice and support through social networks and communities of friends, where the banks don't even exist. UK banks are doing nothing to reach out to customers online and gain their confidence and trust and yet, as I've said so often, this is the best place to build it.

In the UK, there must be something wrong here … and there is.

The fact is that banks should be creating transparency and communicating with customers through mobile and online channels in an honest and open exchange. This is a huge opportunity, not a threat.

The fact is that the UK banks have lost the plot when it comes to marketing and customer relationships. Please get it back and start to focus upon how to reach out to customers through social media and social networking, as well as other remote channels, to rebuild customer confidence.

Meanwhile, if you want to know how to spot a leading bank in the new world of remote finance, look at the ones who got onto Twitter first: Wachovia (18 August 2008); Bank of America (7 January 2009); ING Direct (6 February 2009); Wells Fargo (26 March 2009). These banks already have thousands of Twitter followers.

Banking in a zero margin world (2009)

I know I go on and on and on about Web 2.0 and social media, but I do this because these trends illustrate a fundamental shift in the way we live. The fact I'm blogging here every day, downloading music and film files, connecting globally with all my friends, family and business colleagues through my mobile, laptop, TV and iPod via Facebook, Bebo, MySpace and Cyworld, texting and sharing my life through diggs, flickrs and tweets, means that I'm living differently.

This is what I talk about in workshops that look in-depth at the whole nature of how banking is changing, and I use all of the social network stuff to illustrate the implications.

So a group of bankers attended one of these meetings the other day, and most came back with positive comments except one. He said: "Chris, that was dull. You're just talking about the internet and internet banking. Banking is more than just the internet channel".

I chatted with him a bit and discovered he had got completely the wrong end of the stick. He thought I was just talking about Web 2.0, the internet and social networking online.

I'm not. I'm talking about life and how society is changing through being electronically connected.

The fact that one in four people on this planet can talk to each other in an interactive conversation via a mobile, PC, laptop, Blackberry or other connected device today, is what is changing the world.

That is why life on this planet is different, and it is changing every second of every minute of every day, because of this.

And just as life is different and changing, banking is not the same anymore. In fact, it is becoming unrecognisable. In all areas of banking, we are moving from spreads of 5% or more, to 0.5% or less.

This latter environment is being driven by Moore's Law and the power of the network of the 21st century, as illustrated best by social networking developments in a consumer context because it personalises it.

This network enables everyone globally to be easily connected through cheap, disposable technologies, and that is why it is so disruptive to banks, as shown particularly by the disruptions Zopa, BATS and Chi-X are bringing to bear.

This means that bank legacies of buildings, employee numbers, systems, infrastructures and operations, will need to be continually reviewed, re-evaluated and reconsidered, if we are to compete with the new players. These new players are threatening as they are creating highly competitive services at a tenth of the cost with zero overheads.

That is why I use social media so often to illustrate the future of banking – because you can illustrate how dramatically these technologies are changing the way we live. In this way, I then hope that bankers can start to see how dramatically these technologies are changing the structure of our markets and competition.

It is not about the internet, however ... it is about the way we live, work, compete and communicate.

By the way, I do have an answer about how to make money in a zero margin world.

Give it away for nothing. Give away the commodity stuff – executing, processing, connecting – then find ways to add value that people will pay for. Advice, research, speed, reach, breadth, depth, choice ... that's what Google, Facebook and others build their business upon (and advertising of course!).

Start with what can you give away for nothing that locks people into your business model, then add valuable options to that core free offer that people will pay for.

Meanwhile, the banker who thought I was just talking about the internet has lost his job and been replaced by an avatar.

Tough.

The amazing world of social connectivity (2010)

It's been a while since I did a numbers post on social media, but it's time for an update and there's a great supplement in the *Economist* discussing all things social networking. Here's a summary of the stats.

Social audiences

- Facebook is the globe's largest online social network with over 350 million users;
- Facebook's audience is bigger than any TV network that has ever existed on Earth;
- Were it a nation, Facebook would be the world's third most populous after China and India;
- 70% of its audience is outside the United States;
- Twitter had 58 million web visitors in October 2009;
- Facebook took almost five years to get its first 150m users, but just eight months to double that number;
- LinkedIn has over 58 million members, and it took 16 months to reach its first million users whereas the most recent additional million came on board in only 11 days.

Mobile social

- eMarketer estimate that over 600 million people will use their phones to tap into social networks by 2013, a more-than-fourfold increase on last year's 140 million;
- Facebook has 65 million mobile users.

Social content

- Facebook's users post over 55 million updates a day and share more than 3.5 billion pieces of content with one another every week;
- Over 2.5 billion photos a month are uploaded to Facebook, making it one of the largest photo-sharing sites on the web;
- Facebook has one engineer for every 1.2 million users;
- Facebook has over 1 million developers creating software for it and its online directory contains over 500,000 apps;
- Twitter has spawned over 50,000 apps, including offerings from firms such as Twitpic, which lets people post photos to their Twitter feeds, and Twitscoop, which highlights popular topics being talked about on the service at any moment.

Social revenues

- Facebook does not reveal numbers, but its revenues last year are thought to have been at least $500m and quite possibly more, which helped it to turn cash-flow positive in mid-2009;
- Although user numbers were sharply up last year, the social-networking industry's revenues in America, its biggest advertising market, rose only by a modest 4% to $1.2 billion according to eMarketer, a market research firm;
- That was still an achievement, because the total online advertising market shrank in 2009 and MySpace revenues, the largest share, are thought to have fallen last year.
- This year eMarketer expects revenues to grow by over 7%;
- ComScore found that one in five adverts viewed by American web users last June ran on social networking sites, with MySpace still accounting for the biggest chunk of the total.

Social games

- In 2008 Tencent, the Chinese 'Facebook' which runs QQ coins, listed on the Hong Kong Stock Exchange and reported revenues of just over $1 billion, with $720m coming from online gaming and sales of items such as digital swords and other virtual goods;
- Ning, another social networking tool, is targeting gifts rather than games and launched an initiative in October 2009 that allows people to sell customised digital items to their members. These cost anything from 50 cents to $10, and over 400,000 are being exchanged every month, splitting the profit equally with its customers;
- In the game 'Sorority Life', users complained about the lack of virtual men to date so Playdom quickly introduced some last November – some 10 million of the boyfriends were promptly snapped up with a few players buying as many as 500 boyfriends each; some paid for their digital darlings with virtual credits won in the game, but others stumped up over $5 a time for their beaux;
- Although Asia remains by far the biggest market for digital knick-knacks, Inside Network, a research firm, has estimated that sales of virtual wares in America on many different kinds of websites reached $1 billion last year and could grow to $1.6 billion in 2010;
- ThinkEquity, an investment bank, reckons that revenues in America from social games could hit $2.2 billion by 2012, a big leap from last year's $375m million.
- "The best virtual goods have real currency," says Mark Pincus who runs Zynga, one of the biggest gaming firms on Facebook.

Social marketing

- A survey of 1,000 heavy users of social networks and other digital media conducted in August 2009 by Razorfish, found that 44% of those following brands on Twitter said they did so because of the exclusive deals the firms offered to users;
- One in five tweets mention specific brand names in the updates;
- O2 found that 17% of Britain's small businesses were using Twitter to attract new customers and some believe they have saved around £5,000 ($8,000) a year from other forms of marketing by doing so.

Social hiring

- US Cellular, a telecoms company, says it saved over $1m last year by using a LinkedIn system that produced good candidates for its jobs faster than traditional recruitment channels;
- A survey by CareerBuilder.com of about 2,700 executives in America last year found that 45% of them looked at job candidates' social-network pages as part of their research, and more than a third of those had unearthed information there that put them off hiring someone.

Social not-working

- A survey of 500 small businesses in America conducted by Citibank last October found that most of them had not used online networks at all because they thought they would be a waste of time;
- Morse estimate that personal use of social networks during the working day was costing the British economy almost £1.4 billion ($2.3 billion) a year in lost productivity;

- Nucleus Research, an American firm, concluded that if companies banned employees from using Facebook while at work, their productivity would improve by 1.5%.
- A survey of 1,400 CIOs by Robert Half Technology last year found that only 1/10th gave employees full access to networks during the day, and many were blocking Facebook and Twitter altogether.

(...)

Meanwhile, if you like this sort of thing a lot, then here's a few more social media numbers, this time from this year's World Economic Forum (WEF):

- WEF reached a worldwide audience of 430 million readers online through the use of social networks this year;
- Facebook ran real-time pulses, polling over 200,000 people and bringing their views into the discussions;
- WEF has over 6,300 fans on Facebook;
- Webcasts of public sessions on Livestream reaching a cumulated audience of over 210,000 viewers;
- News conferences were seen by over 70,000 people, and they could put questions to panellists via Twitter and Facebook;
- Over 250 participants and 120 journalists continuously sharing their impressions on Twitter;
- A Twitterwall allowed participants to see a running micro-commentary on the meeting as it progressed;
- 'Davos', 'WEF' and 'WorldEconomicForum' were mentioned 30,000 times on Twitter;
- 1,551,130 people are following the Forum on Twitter (http://twitter.com/davos);
- The Davos Debates on YouTube (http://www.youtube.com/davos) have been watched over 600,000 times.

The march of mobile social connectivity (2009)

The rise and rise of social media and social networks is illustrated well by the annual report produced by media and branding firm Universal McCann. They've been tracking social media for a while and each year produce a study of what's happening.

The first study was performed in September 2006 looking at 7,500 internet users in 15 countries, increasing in 2009 to 22,729 active internet users – those who use the net at least every other day – in 38 countries.

The most recent survey took place between November 2008 and March 2009. The headline is that increasing numbers of internet users are much more comfortable within the social media and micro-blogging environment, and particularly on their mobile telephone.

The survey notes a major surge in mobile internet access, with 17% of active internet users now online on the move as well as at home.

Can a billion people be wrong? (2008)

During the last year, we've all enjoyed the rise of social media and social networking, with many of us now happily Twittering, Facebooking, Beboing, StudiVZing, MySpacing, Cyworlding, Mixiing, QQing, or whatever takes your fancy.

In fact, the numbers are quite incredible. Considering most of these sites had virtually no users in 2006, the fact that they now have about 230 million registered users with MySpace, 75 million with Facebook, and about 250 million for the rest, you have an awful lot of socially networked people.

In a press release from Comscore in January 2008, the figures speak for themselves:

> "The number of worldwide visitors to social networking sites has grown 34 percent in the past year to 530 million, representing approximately 2 out of every 3 Internet users. MySpace and Facebook are in a tight battle for the global leadership position, each attracting more than 100 million visitors per month."

Two out of every three internet users are socially networking online. That's a lot of people.

And Comscore's figures do not include what I consider to be the planet's biggest social network, QQ. QQ is a Chinese network run by Tencent, a mobile network carrier. Maybe that's why they are left out of Comscore's figures, because they are mobile based, but QQ has 300 million users.

In fact, if you add in all the mobile network social capabilities, such as Twitter, you have over a billion people networking socially through electronic media.

That's one in five people on the planet. That's a helluva lot of people.

The next boom starts in ... 2014? Harnessing the power of the network for growth (2009)

For two years we will be in flat or negative growth, for three years slow growth and then, in 2014, fast growth supported by a boom of new web technologies.

So if your management does not get the next generation technologies. If your management does not see the fact that business models are being created with technologies that cost 1/1000th of your costs, tell them that some companies are running businesses for £3 per day that would have cost them £3,000 per day a decade ago.

Wake them up by telling them that Facebook had only 6 million users in 2006, 60 million in 2007 and, today, has over 140 million. Tell them that YouTube generates more hours of viewing for most people, than traditional TV. Tell them that some bloggers report and manage more news with more distribution and readership than some newspapers. And that anyone can create these global reach capabilities from their homes.

Therefore, sticking to old tried-and-tested structures and operations was good for businesses when businesses were slow to change, but will kill businesses in the next five years as business is now in fast-cycle change.

In 2014, we will be in another growth cycle. A more sombre one, with very different financial instruments and services, and with banks that are far more checked and regulated than ever before, but it will be another growth cycle. Those firms who harness the power of the network will be the ones that achieve the fastest growth in that next cycle.

Chapter 2 Social media's challenges

Introduction

Although social banking is on the horizon today, it is not mainstream as mentioned. This is in part due to bank's inertia, but also down to the newness of this media and its untested and unproven nature. In other words, it's risky. You only have to look at Facebook's ever-changing privacy rules, or lack of privacy if you prefer, to realise that social media and networks may, if anything, undermine the very nature of banking: as in, avoiding risk. Nevertheless, these challenges are just learning cycles on the road towards the next stage of communications evolution and should not be taken as a barrier, but rather an opportunity. An opportunity to improve bank's relationships and the customer's experience.

Integrating social media into the organisation (2010)

The path to integration of social media into the institution is a tough challenge. Firstly, organisations understand that this is an issue requiring total commitment across the organisation, but achieving such is difficult because finding someone who can garner that support is a challenge. Secondly, brands in general are starting to understand that social media is a medium they can't 'spin' – that is, customers are largely in control – and that is worrying, particularly in the current environment where FIs are facing significant perception challenges at large.

Individually, we know that it is inevitable that social media will be integrated into our business, but our organisations are looking for direction. The difficulty is that there is no one size fits all solution. Each of the popular social networking sites works in different ways, so we need strategies that reflect this. The survey showed, for example, that LinkedIn is a far better tool for business-to-business discussions and for promotion of services to professional individuals, such as priority banking and wealth management. For general brand marketing, Facebook is an effective tool, but our respondents wouldn't use Facebook for banking contacts or LinkedIn for private and personal socialising. So banks must target effectively if they are to get the socialisation of finance right. The strategy needs to be localised and involves pay-per-click embedded advertising as well as sponsored groups and consumer support.

Identity and security issues (2009)

It concerns me how careful or careless people are, when using networked worlds in managing their identity.

I'll take Facebook as the example here, as that's the one I'm familiar with, but I'm sure most other social media applications are the same.

First, there's the connecting with complete strangers. This is best illustrated by a study by the internet security firm Sophos. Sophos ran a joke last year on Facebook, and were surprised to find that most people accepted them as a friendly connection, even though people did not know who was reaching out to them. If they checked out the stranger's profile, it just had a picture of a plastic frog on it, and yet they still accepted this stranger's connection. This just reflects basic human nature. We want to be popular so if someone wants to be our friend, oh, yes please!

Second, is the ability to easily see everyone's profiles if you know how. The simplest thing to do is to join a network, such as London, and then look around. You can read a lot of people's profiles and they don't even know it because, when they joined the London network, they forgot to set their profile on the London Network to 'private'. Result: everyone in London can see your profile whenever they want.

That can have some serious implications, as demonstrated by Crystal Palace teenage footballer, Ashley-Paul Robinson.

Ashley-Paul had his first full team game for Crystal Palace in April and is a promising star for the future. However, he posted details of his forthcoming try-out for Fulham, an arch-rival football team, on his Facebook profile without realising that, because he was part of the London network, 2.7 million people could read it. One of the people who read this news was the Crystal Palace team manager, Neil Warnock, who has told Ashley-Paul he is a Faceberk and that his Crystal Palace future was over.

Finally, I've found a new quirk in Facebook. If you annotate on a friend's photograph, then you are allowing all of your friends to see your friend's photo album.

This can best be illustrated by the example of my friend John, who knows Jane. I don't know Jane and have no connection with her. However, John decides to write a note on Jane's photo saying, 'Nice piccie'. Because John makes that comment, I can now see all of Jane's photograph album and all of the comments in that album. Even though I don't know Jane.

The average Facebook user has 164 friends. So, in practice, this means that I can potentially see the details of my 164 friends x their 164 friends, who I do not know. That's over 25,000 people who are now exposed to me through the network. Not just exposed as individuals, but their lives, friends, habits and social world.

The bottom line is that through Facebook, I potentially have access to millions of people's profiles, lives, friends, boyfriends, girlfriends, brothers, sisters, fathers, daughters, mothers, sons ... their birth dates, home town, place they live now, where they work, their mobile telephone numbers, email addresses, habits and thoughts.

And if I know how to do this in Facebook, I am sure that I could find similar exposures in MySpace, Bebo, Badoo, QQ and more.

For the true friends I have out there who I enjoy networking with, this is fantastic. For the hundreds of strangers I now have access to through the network, this is dangerous. In fact, it's so dangerous that I believe yes, a billion people can be wrong. A billion people, one in five people on this planet, may be giving away their identities and more in the name of social fun.

So what does this mean for banks?

Well, banks really need to start raising this issue, in the same way as phishing and spam. This would mean placing signs everywhere on bank internet and mobile services, saying something like:

"If your identity is compromised and we find this is a result of your usage of social networking sites such as Facebook or MySpace, you will be liable for any losses incurred. You may not realise but your identity can be traced through these internet sites if people can access your profile. Your profile can be accessed by all of those you are connected with and, quite often, their connections. Equally, anyone on a network, such as the London network, maybe able to see your profile. That equates to almost 3 million people who can see your birthday, email address, friends and family, and anything else you place on these social media. Therefore, we recommend you do the following best practices ..." – and so on.

But there is more to this than just identity theft issues. In fact, for a bank, there is far more concern about what these sites could mean for social engineering fraud and theft.

For example, I regularly find details of tellers and customer service representatives for various banks. I can even target the banks I want to have a go at, by name. Each of these banks have staff socially networking online and, even though I have never met any of them, they give me all of the information I need about their lifestyles and contact details. I just wonder what would happen if I went down to their local bar and said I had their brother or sister, mother or father, son or daughter, held at home at gunpoint unless they help me rob the bank.

I don't have their family or friends at gunpoint ... I just know their names and details. Just as I knew where they drank, when and how often. It's all on their profile.

Just a thought.

More on the dangers of social networks (2009)

Social networks not only offer the opportunity to create a new way of reaching the customer but, more importantly possibly, the danger of customers being compromised through the information they share.

(...)

This social networking, sharing and connecting of individual's private information has therefore been one of the biggest dangers of these new networks, but has not received much headline grabbing news from the financial community. Probably because we ignore it.

Luckily therefore, the dangers of social networks are being tackled by governments. Last week, 49 States in the US agreed important safeguards with Facebook and MySpace over privacy concerns. These include:

- Restricting advertising to only those age groups who should see such adverts, e.g. youngsters will not be offered Hooch and Marlboro ads;
- Remove groups that could imply that they are related to paedophilia, bullying or other inappropriate content; and
- Sending warning messages when a child is in danger of giving personal information to an adult.

The thing is that all of these government efforts are far more targeted at restricting pornographic predators, rather than financial fraudsters. So it may be a while yet before the financial community is willing to take the risk and make full use of social networks.

A beginner's guide to robbery in the 21st century (2009)

I know I shouldn't publish this, as some folks might take note for illicit purposes, but what I'm writing is nothing new. It's already well-known by the criminal fraternity, so I might as well share it with you. It's also well known in the risk and security community, but they don't seem to make it as clear as I'd like it to be.

What am I talking about?

Social engineering. The number one method of committing a robbery in the 21st century.

Here are a few examples of how easily social engineering works.

Example #1

(...)

I look around Facebook and find the details of a person. They have given their email address as sxodavies@aol.com and, as I look around their Facebook profile I find their mom is called Ruth, their dad is David, they have a sister and brother, Carly and Robert (Bobby), and a pet dog called Scamps. Their favourite rock star is Christina Aguilera and their favourite celebrity Ashton Kutcher. I go to AOL and enter username as sdavies and then try variations of passwords from Ruth, David, Carly, Robert, Bobby, Scamps, Christina and Ashton. It works as most folks use a password that is a family member's name, a pet or a personality they like.

Result: identity compromised in less than 10 minutes.

Example #2

I want to gain access to someone's account so I begin by using Facebook as above. This time, I have found a variety of details about the individual, including the fact that their name is Suzanne and they have a number of financial accounts and investments. I've discovered this information because I'm quietly watching what they're emailing, both sending and receiving, and they have no idea I'm watching or accessing.

Eventually, I know enough to be confident to call their bank, and I get my female friend to make the call and pretend to be Suzanne:

"Hello, my name's Suzanne Davies and I'd like to move £650 to my savings account."

My friend struggles with some of the security questions and, not wanting to be rude, the call centre person helps them out with a little prompting, as Suzanne seems to know most of her personal information. So she gets to know the postcode, the place of birth and other information. However, she gets to the personal security question, "what's your mother's maiden name", and my friend says that she's been interrupted and will call back.

This goes on several times until my female friend has all the information needed to transfer funds.

Result: identity stolen within half a day.

These are just a few examples from hundreds and, although you may think me a little risky in posting them, if anyone wanted to try these techniques then they're all out there, known and can be easily demonstrated.

This is because all of the stories above are true stories and all of them rely upon one fundamental characteristic: the villain is bold, confident and assertive, whilst the rest of us are trusting, unchallenging and supportive.

That, my friends, is the total basis of social engineering for robbing in the 21st century.

In other words, most deliberate theft relies upon the fact that most of us are trusting. We don't protect vital information because we trust people. We fear challenging someone who seems to know what they're doing because we trust they should be honourable and ok.

All you need is a little information, a lot of confidence and then prey on people's trust. This is the stuff of *The Real Hustle* and there are many other examples of how this works in practice. In fact, robbers haven't really changed for years, as Raffles, the fictional gentleman thief from over a hundred years ago, stole with the same trickster's confidence. It's just far easier to be Raffles today than it was a century ago.

A robber who is confident and knows a few facts, can blag their way through anything. A bit like the way Chris Tucker in *Rush Hour* or Eddie Murphy in *Beverly Hills Cop* can convince a bar room full of tough guys that they're a cop with a licence, when all they are is a guy with a flashy badge, if you look the part, act the part and believe you are the part, then you can swing anything.

So, there you have it. I can easily pass myself off as anyone I want to be, as long as I believe.

Somebody stop me!

I'm sorry, you are firewalled out (2009)

I regularly run workshops on the future of banking. Part of the workshop explores the implications of virtual worlds and social networking on bank services, and what the world of banking might look like five years from now as a result. Yep, you guessed it, we talk about Entropia, Second Life, Habbo Hotel and Club Penguin; we also talk about Facebook, MySpace, Bebo, Cyworld, Mixi and Badoo.

The normal reaction at the end of such discussions is: "Chris, I never knew about any of this. It's fascinating. Is our bank doing anything?" which kinda amazes me, (a) that they don't know about it and (b) that they don't know if their bank is doing anything.

Now the fact is that very few banks are doing much in this world of any note.

(...)

I started to wonder why it was that so many people "never knew any of this was happening"? I mean, even the folks who use social networking didn't know a lot of what was really happening. This is because they have a Facebook page "because my kids use it" and although they therefore are aware of Facebook and stuff, they admit that they *don't get it!*

I discovered the answer as to why most don't get it about 18 months ago.

I was at an annual kick-off internal conference for a client in October 2006, where the CEO of this major global organisation was addressing the audience. This company has offices in almost every country, has a multi-billion dollar turnover, and is one that everyone would recognise. They are also one of the most strategically-led companies in the world, always ahead of the pack.

He began by saying how astounded he was that Google had just paid $1.65 billion to buy YouTube. He was astounded because, as the most strategic company in the world, how could he not be aware of a company that was worth $1.65 billion? He had never heard of YouTube.

So he called all of his direct reports into a meeting and said: "How many of you are aware of YouTube?" No-one raised a hand. He said, "Well, this morning Google paid $1.65 billion for them and so, as the most strategic company in the world, it is to our shame that we don't know what they do. Let's find out."

At this point, he switched on his PC and typed in www.youtube.com. The computer buzzed away for a few seconds and then spat out the answer, "The corporate firewall does not allow you access to this service, please talk to the systems administrator if you are having a problem."

This is the irony of the modern world, as nearly every large, traditional organisation is firewalled out. Strategists, marketers, technologists, bankers, consultants, governments and more are all missing out on the most fundamental changes to our world because it is invisible to them.

This is why people tell me "Chris, I never knew about any of this", because it is hidden away from them. They spend their days working for companies that stop them from being involved with what they see as follies, gimmicks and time-wasting websites, because the employees should be working. That's why we employ them.

The employees then go home in the evening to become humans, and the last thing they want to do is waste time using websites that they don't know why they exist because they want to play with their kids, eat dinner and have time with family and friends.

The world of today is passing by the generation of yesterday because the management dictate policies of yesterday to the world of today.

What the hell will they be doing tomorrow?

The YouTube consumer wins (2009)

Social media certainly puts power back into the hands of the consumer, instead of the banks. Ann Minch of California posted an angry little video about Bank of America's policies on her credit card in mid-September, saying that Bank of America upped her credit card interest rates to 30% with no notice, and wouldn't discuss why.

So what? Well, it mattered as her little rant got linked to by blogs and newswires globally such that, as I write this, her video has been viewed over 430,000 times. And guess what? According to Huffington Post, Ann was contacted by a Bank of America official the other day "to talk a little about my personal financial situation so we can negotiate some kind of agreement in regard to my existing credit card account," she said.

The executive "tried to get me to agree to 16.99 percent and I said, 'No, nope, I believe because you guys are getting your money from the Fed at zero percent interest... that 12.99 percent is a more than generous profit margin for you guys.' So he did finally agree to that and he also agreed to send me that in writing."

The power of social media in action.

Global, Blogal, Social, Glocial (2009)

In this worldwide web of global wonders, I'm getting fairly cheesed off with the number of social networks I'm now getting involved with. From Facebook to LinkedIn to Plaxo to Bebo, they're all starting to mind-meld into one. Add in Habbo Hotel, Second Life, Entropia and all the other virtual worlds, and you almost lose the will to live trying to keep up with them all.

No wonder Ben Elton has just produced a comic book, *Blind Faith,* based upon the idea that those who don't join in social media are jailed.

I must admit, in a similar fashion, I've started adding some frivolous banter to my Facebook and twitters lately, such as "Chris is up", "Chris is down", "Chris is square", "Chris is round", and even "Chris is masticating" *(read very carefully).*

Oh, it's all such social fun with my global crowd of friends and strangers. However, there can only be enough room for just so many of these sites, so where does it stop?

Everyone wants to get in on this bandwagon. The trouble is that the bandwagon rapidly gets full and overflowing with too many, and so we will see some falling off over time, both in this social finance and wider social networking world.

The other issue is that, with so many of these websites out there, you can get stuck in them for the day. Between socialising in virtual online business worlds and blogging about them, there's no time left in the day to do anything worthwhile!

So I'm giving up all of these social networks to live in the real world.

Is this the real world ... or is this just fantasy?

Chapter 3 Twitter, Facebook and other social networks

Introduction

The newness of networks shouldn't be a reason for not experimenting with them as, unlike in olden days when new ventures took years to gain critical mass, these ventures take months. For example, social gaming firm Zynga found their Facebook game Farmville went from zero users to over 60 million – yes, that's 60,000,000 – in just three months during the summer of 2009. Facebook has grown from nothing in 2006 to one of the world's third largest communities, with a population of 500 million people, in just four years. Twitter had its first tweet in 2006 and reached its 10 billionth tweet in February 2010 and its 20 billionth in July 2010. This stuff grows fast, and its all about the viral effect of the network, as in the more who network, the more who network. That is why this stuff is important to you, me, banks and the world.

Why banks should focus upon Twitter (2009)

Twitter is the new social networking focal point, due to the rapidly growing numbers of fans of their service. Now there are many folks asking questions about Twitter, as it gains momentum.

For example, in the last few days, Paul Penrose at Finextra asks: "What's the point of Twitter?" whilst, in an article for *Marketing Week*, Andrew Harrison claims that Twitter is the emperor's new clothes.

The thing is that, as demonstrated by the latter view, it is easy to pour scorn on things we don't understand or know how to use effectively, but Twitter is rapidly emerging as a major source of financial innovation and should not be ignored.

For example, were any of you the ones who thought that a mobile phone was for yuppies, a Blackberry was a waste of time or wonder why anyone would want to text message? How wrong you can be, and, if you have those attitudes, you can easily miss the biggest wave of change we have ever seen in our times.

That wave of change is illustrated by every other person on the planet now having access to a mobile phone and millions of text messages being used for payments.

The thing is that many of us try to shun things we don't understand, don't like or are scared of. But that's wrong. If people are embracing a new technology – and millions have chirped over to tweet lately – then it warrants understanding.

In my case, I didn't get Twitter as I'm not a mobile junkie and that's who I thought it was designed for, but I've now discovered lots of net-based tools for Twitter – such as Tweetdeck and Monitter – and it's become my essential text message service for the internet.

And sure, you get the odd person (did I say, 'odd'?) who posts stuff like "just eaten a sandwich", or "been to the toilet" ... and they're the ones who probably rang folks with their mobile in the 1990s saying "I'm on the train" or "I can't hear you, you're breaking up".

You see, there are things that Twitter's fantastic for and, for those who are interested in trying to keep up to speed with information overload, having your mates say "another bank bankruptcy" or "look at this article on social media" is really useful.

Equally, for catching customer dialogue and responding it can be terrific too, as Commonwealth Bank of Australia (CBA) found out this week when a customer posted an angry tweet.

The client was going through a lengthy mortgage process with CBA and was fed up with the wait for final approval which might mean they'd lose their house purchase. So they tweeted their frustrations and, within an hour, had a CBA customer service rep tweet back, sort out their issue and deliver great customer satisfaction. Now there's service for you.

So I can't handle these folks who rain on someone's parade just because they don't understand it. Mr. Harrison's article, for example, claims Twitter has 1.2 million users worldwide and this was published in the week of 26th March 2009. The actual number is 7 million and rising. He does qualify this to be 'active' users and, whether it's 1 or 7 million, it's enough to get attention.

After all, we probably dismissed PayPal when they had 1 million active users and today they have over 70 million. It doesn't take long.

Bottom line: to diss this stuff sounds like someone saying television will wipe out cinema or the internet is just for pornography and gambling.

From a financial market viewpoint, the question is whether there is opportunity to monetise and grow business through such services.

Although Twitter is new, there are already many financial oriented sites that are growing around it, such as TwitPay, Twollars, Twipper, Harvest, Xpenser, Tweetwhatyouspend, StockTwits and FXTwits.

These are all sites offering some form of payment or social finance service through Twitter, and I have to thank J J Hornblass at Bank Innovation for these tips, as he has been keeping a pulse on this activity.

Wesabe and other social finance websites are also integrating with Twitter, so they think it's important, as do some innovative banks, such as Wachovia, Bank of America, ING Direct, and Wells Fargo.

So the real reasons Twitter is important are:

- It's an SMS across all platforms, mobile and internet;
- It fits with the Attention Deficit Disorder, or ADD generation (which includes me) ;
- It's got lots of add-ons for great functionality and usability;
- It works;

- It's useful;
- It's quick and easy;
- It's good.

What more could you want?

Oh, and if still not convinced, here's 10 reasons to use Twitter from Dave Lee, a technology journalist for the BBC and co-editor of the BBC Internet Blog:

1. You'll know about stuff before everyone else does;
2. You can use it to find out what people think... about anything;
3. You can find people who like what you do;
4. You can use it to get help.;
5. It can transform your career;
6. You can campaign for good;
7. You can talk directly to people in power;
8. You can read stuff you'd never normally have found;
9. You can use it to save heaps of time;
10. MC Hammer is on there.

Banks can ignore Twitter no longer (2010)

Two years ago Twitter was unheard of. Although Twitter started beta testing their concept in 2006, it is largely agreed that it didn't formally launch until April 2007. Since then Twitter has taken off by storm – globally, in the US and in Australia, Twitter ranks as the 12th most popular website by traffic, in the UK it ranks in the top 10, and in most of the EU it ranks in the top 30 or 50 websites. It took Facebook four years to achieve the same impact; so social media adoption is definitely speeding up, not slowing down.

Twitter is an excellent research tool. We would say that this medium in its current form would probably yield more data than your best of breed focus groups and customer satisfaction surveys if it can be harnessed correctly. When it comes to Twitter it is all about listening. Our recent social media survey showed that consumers would use social media first to ask other customers about their experience with your brand, rather than engaging with your brand directly.

Arguing about Twitter is a waste of time (2009)

There have been various arguments about Twitter in the last few months and whether the alerts tool is useful or not. I started one debate a while ago and now there is another one (maybe).

First, let me set the record straight before folks think I'm a puritanically obsessed Twitterati. At a personal level, I am a fan of Twitter; I'm not a big networker on Facebook; I don't like Second Life; and most social networking online is dross.

People misinterpret what you say and think and they also distort the facts to suit their own views of the world (don't we all?).

The reason why I write about these themes so often, however, is that, at a business level, I think all of these developments are changing our world socially and commercially. That is why they are important.

Often people cannot see this because they are constrained by their assumptions of how they see this world. The best example of this is that I wrote my monthly column for one journal recently, and they edited a key line from what I wrote:

"Twitter is used mainly by those over 35" to: "Twitter is used mainly by those under 35".

So I sent the editor a note saying that not only did he edit my column to oblivion so it didn't read well, but also changed a critical fact, namely that the majority of Twitter users are over the age of 35:

- 20 per cent of all tweeters in Britain are over the age of 55, compared with 12 per cent of Facebook users;
- 45- to 54-year-olds are 36% more likely to be using the site on average; and
- The majority of the 10 million Twitter users worldwide are aged 35 or older.

This is therefore a good audience for bankers.

These assumptions about our world, e.g., Twitter/Facebook/ social networks is for youngsters, demonstrates that many people, especially the digital aliens and immigrants, don't believe what is factually correct and so they change the whole meaning of it to suit their own interpretations and false views of the world.

This is a mistake. Not only are Twitter users older, but the majority of Facebook users are middle-life females sharing their family with their extended family who often live in other towns, cities or even countries.

This is how these tools are changing our lives socially and, soon, commercially. Just as the internet has changed our lives, and Amazon and iTunes have wiped out traditional book and record stores, this new revolution is doing the same for how we communicate and relate to each other.

Back to Twitter.

Many people aren't too sure what Twitter is about and having tried it, think they get it and don't see why it's useful, so they then pour doubt on its usefulness. I did the same until I found the way to incorporate this tool into my work and social life.

You see, I prefer networking socially in the real world. I like my life and don't need a second one.

And Jonathan Ross popping up on Twitter on a regular basis saying: "Mr. Pickles has just been sick" just makes me think of the words of an old movie star: "Frankly, my dear, I don't give a damn".

That's why I think social networking online is dross, because I prefer social networking in real life. That's why I don't need a second life and I'm verbose enough as it is without Twitter. But Twitter, Facebook and Second Life are useful for augmenting my real life with social tools when I am unable to network in the real world due to distance, time or capacity.

And what I really do care about is future business, commerce and banking.

Focusing on the future is where I sit firmly, strategically and seeking every opportunity to maximise revenues and profitability for the future.

I am not arguing about Twitter and whether it's worth it or not. I don't care about Twitter in itself. What I care about is how micro-blogging and sharing of URLs on an enterprise and globalised basis, changes news sharing and knowledge.

That's what Twitter does today. It's the RSS2.0 of the internet. Tomorrow, it could be Digger, Deliciouser or Grunter. I don't care.

My key observation is not so much about Twitter, Second Life and Facebook as internet crazes, which they are.

The fact is that all of these have a sound base for future commerce however, which is social communications providing an ability through new channels to create commercial opportunities.

This is why I am so adamant about this stuff – not the transient nature of a craze for Twitter, Facebook or Second Life, but the long-term nature of what these things can possibly do for us and our business/planet.

In case anyone is in any doubt about where I'm coming from, I come from the land of missed opportunities. I come from the land of thinking Microsoft's share price peaked in 1993. I come from the land of "who needs a mobile phone"? I come from the land of "Google is just Altavista and Yahoo! and won't last".

And, as a financier, banker, investor or whatever you or I might be, if you see an opportunity this good, then take it.

Oh yes, and what is that opportunity? At a time when bankers are trusted less than tobacco firms, communicate openly, honestly and transparently with customers to regain business before someone else does.

Meantime, arguing about whether Twitter is worthwhile or not is about as useful as a f*rt in a space suit.

A few bank CEO's agree with me. Here's ANZ's CEO Brian Hartzer on why he Twitters:

"There's no doubt that social networking is not only growing in take-up, but in importance as a channel. Twitter is unlike any other social media vehicle because its immediate, honest and no-nonsense environment really allows you to feel the pulse of the community."

Neil Robinson of LANZen also pointed to a useful article on David Knapp of Bank of America, who runs their Twitter service, BofA Help:

"I contacted him a few days ago (via Twitter) ... He responded within 10 minutes of my tweet, got my contact information from me, and forwarded it onto a BoA rep in my area. I missed their first call, but before I even had a chance to call them back, I saw that both my fees had been refunded."

Are Twitter and other social media are no longer relevant? (2009)

I don't think so. Twitter is an evolving medium which some people like and find useful for knowledge sharing whilst others find it of no interest at all.

This is why I take the view that Twitter and other social media need to be considered in context, as these tools are useful for communications, but this is an evolution not a static moment.

Twitter, Facebook, MySpace and more could come and go as quickly as a politician's seat in government, but their model of communication is here to stay. After all, these tools are just replacing Instant Messaging, Friendster and Friends Reunited with easier ways of socialising. In another few years, they may have been replaced again.

And we really need to see these tools in the context of the evolution of the web and other technologies. For example, a decade ago AOL was one of the biggest providers of access to the online community and became so big they acquired Time Warner. Today, AOL is dead meat and broadband communications carriers along with Yahoo! lead the world. But just for now.

A decade ago, eBay ruled the commercial community. Today, it is a dwindling flame. Over a decade ago, Netscape ruled the world. Then Microsoft extinguished their fire. Now Firefox and Chrome are trying to do the same to Internet Explorer.

Therefore, we need to see the context of our web evolution and consider that what we are really seeing a phase of innovation around how we connect to each other.

This would mean that the first phase of the web was all about commerce, knowledge and search – eBay, Amazon, Expedia, Google.

The second phase is all about communications, relationships and reactive media – Facebook, MySpace, Bebo, Second Life, Twitter ... and this phase has not completed yet, so we have no idea who the Amazons and Googles will be for this generation.

There will then be the next phase, which will, in my view, be all about meaning, context and proactive media. Connecting me with people is great, but I want you to give my connection context. Who is the most worthy for me to connect to and through what media? When I want to buy things, recommend where to buy them. Look at my way of living digitally and tell me how to live better electronically.

This web is already close, and we can already see the strands of such proactive media. Plaxo, LinkedIn, Facebook and more now tell me who I might want to connect to. They recommend to me. iTunes, Amazon and more tell me what I might want to buy. They recommend to me. Mint, Wesabe and more now tell me how I might want to organise my finances. They recommend to me.

Take this on one generation, and the next web will see the current tone replaced by proactive recommendation engines. These engines will seamlessly work in my life via my mobile telephone, my web homepages and my television and more.

Then Twitter, Facebook, Amazon and other great first and second generation internet names may again wither and die or flourish and become reborn.

In the meantime, this means that denigrating the transient moments of media that spark and disappear is just pointless when the real focus is on what these transient sparks do to our way of living, socialising, buying and selling.

That's the real point.

Meantime, those who think Web 2.0 is dead are just talking recycling materials … in other words, rubbish.

Is the social web party over? (2009)

I keep reading reports of Second Life being an overhyped piece of dead meat, and now get the same vibes about Twitter and more.

In the latest round of discussions, James Gardner and Ron Shevlin both question the worthiness of Twitter for banking, whilst an interesting survey by Purewire found that millions of Twitterati never actually tweet. Purewire managed to analyse about 7 million Twitter user profiles and found that many Twitter users abandoned their accounts shortly after creating them:

- 40% of Twitter users have not tweeted since their first day on Twitter, which means that the account was most likely created and subsequently forgotten about; and
- Around 25% are not following anyone, while two-thirds are following less than 10 people, which probably means that the account was created but is not being used regularly.

The data also shows that most users find Twitter useful for receiving information, rather than sending or interacting:

- Over a third of users have not posted a single tweet and almost 80% have less than 10 tweets;
- Around a third have no followers whilst 80% have fewer than 10; and
- 50% are following more people than follow them whilst another 30% follow the same number of people who follow them.

A brief review of (Oz) bank twittering (2009)

For some time, we've seen Twitter emerge as a communications channel and wondered what it means for banks. This morning, I gained a good insight as I was alerted to some dialogue between UBank, a division of the National Bank of Australia (NAB), and someone who made a comment about them.

It all began with this tweet from a chap called Simon:

> 'Wow, user experience of signing up to NAB sub-brand UBank online is surprisingly slick!'

Nice compliment Simon, and one that did not go unnoticed by UBank:

> 'RT@shremozle Wow, user of signing up to NAB sub-brand UBank online is surprisingly slick! --> Thanks for that *blush* (MH)'

Obviously UBank are using twitterbots to track and spot whenever their name is mentioned in a tweet. Then I thought: "mmmm, does Simon feel a bit like he's being stalked?" No matter. It prompted me to look at UBank's tweets and a couple of others gave me a slightly different picture:

> 'Thanks to those waiting patiently on hold at our 24x7 Direct Banking Centre, we apologise for the longer than usual wait, it's very busy (MH)'
>
> '@smiffytech Do you mind dropping us a note with the specific address input challenges we caused you?'
>
> '@dkam We're onto that, should be fixed in the next 24 hrs.
>
> Thanks for your feedback, greatly appreciated (MH)

As can be seen, an actively twittering bank which uses Twitter for customer service, dialogue and debate, provides a transparent insight into their operations. The good, the bad and the ugly. I quite liked that, although most banks would feel pretty uncomfortable with that level of transparency, which is why most look more like Westpac, which has protected its tweets.

No wonder Westpac have no followers ... or maybe their followers are the only Westpac customers who, so far, have worked out there's a thing called Twitter out there?

In between are a number of other examples of how banks and financial firms use twitter.

For example, Twitter is useful for keeping track of the competition. Mind you, I'm not so sure about promoting the competition, as Commonwealth Bank of Australia (CBA) seem to be. CBA's Twitter page for Generation Y customers – YMoneyMatters – appears to be promoting customers to follow the competition, in the form of NAB's Rob Findlay. Rob is a manager of customer experiences at NAB, and writes the Bank Channel blog which YMoneyMatters recommends folks to follow.

Good for you, CBA!

I also thought CBA understood Twitter, as they were one of the first banks to hit the headlines for using Twitter for customer service. They supposedly had spotted a customer with mortgage troubles and solved them within a day, thanks to an eagle-eyed Twittering customer service rep.

I say 'supposedly' because, afterwards, it turns out that the person with the mortgage problem worked for the paper that published the story, so it was again an example of a story that is not as simple as it seemed.

And although CBA are promoting to youth (who don't use Twitter), trying to find their general Twitter page is hard ... as there doesn't appear to be one.

Mind you, many other Australian banks are trying to use Twitter to promote their ideas about money to their customers, with Rabobank's Raboplus service being one of the most notable.

Similarly SmartyPig, which runs in Australia in a joint venture with ANZ, has a lot to offer in terms of inspiration and ideas. Although I wasn't so impressed with the inactivity of their ANZ partner, who seem to take most of their tweets from SmartyPig. Don't you have your own voice, ANZ?

Meantime, my favourite bank tweet has to be St. George's Bank which, like UBank, stalks customers for mentions of their brand. So when dandilionseed had this conversation therefore:

> 'I think I just punched a hole in someone's confidence by refusing to hug him in the middle of the city with so many ppl staring!'

'@dandilionseed What did he say afterward?'

'Nothing – (his body language said everything though) he was dressed in a dragon suit advertising for St George's Bank',

they could not help but respond:

'@dandilionseed Poor Happy Dragon! Next time give him a hug, he loves it :)'

BTW, as I know none of these people, it just goes to show how transparent our 24*7 modern world of tweets really is!

Anyways, in summary, you have bank twittering that shows it can be a great:

- Knowledge sharing system;
- Customer and competitor tracking system;
- Customer service tool; and
- Promotional information system, all in real time.

Inside Twitter (2009)

As Twitter is still a hot topic for some, there's a really interesting survey that has just been released by social media analytics firm Sysomos. After analysing information disclosed on 11.5 million Twitters accounts in July, they discovered that:

- 72.5% of all users joined between January 1 and May 31 2009;
- 85.3% of all Twitter users post less than one update per day;
- 21% of users have never posted a Tweet;
- 93.6% of users have less than 100 followers, while 92.4% follow less than 100 people;
- 5% of Twitter users account for 75% of all activity;
- New York has the most Twitters users, followed by Los Angeles, Toronto, San Francisco and Boston, while

Detroit was the fast-growing city over the first five months of 2009;

- More than 50% of all updates are published using tools, mobile and Web-based, other than Twitter.com;
- TweetDeck is the most popular non-Twitter.com tool with 19.7% market share;
- There are more women on Twitter (53%) than men (47%);
- Of the people who identify themselves as marketers, 15% follow more than 2,000 people. This compares with 0.29% of overall Twitter users who follow more than 2,000 people.

Twitter is not for teens, Morgan Stanley (2009)

It surprises me to read that a teen intern's paper on social media has created a massive flurry of interest in Morgan Stanley and their clients' middle-aged management teams.

> "The *Financial Times* reported today that the US investment bank's European media analysts asked Matthew Robson, a (15-year old) intern from a London school, to write a report on teenagers' likes and dislikes.
>
> "His report, that dismissed Twitter and described online advertising as pointless, proved to be 'one of the clearest and most thought-provoking insights we have seen – so we published it', said Edward Hill-Wood, head of Morgan Stanley's European media team.
>
> "'We've had dozens and dozens of fund managers, and several CEOs, e-mailing and calling all day.' He said the note had generated five or six times more responses than the team's usual research."

The reason it surprises me that this is news is that it is pretty obvious stuff for those who study or know about this space.

This is because Twitter is a real-time newsfeed service that people who like news – you and I – find indispensable after a short while. Sure, you can share social news via Twitter, but it lacks the personalisation of other social networking tools. That is why Twitter is not for teens. Teens would rather invest in building a cool profile of themselves that is personalised.

This is why Bebo, MySpace and Facebook work well for them. These social network sites incorporate the status updates and, in the case of Facebook, are becoming more real time ... but Twitter just allows short messaging. Sure with Twitpics and other things, you can link to more of your social life, but a short message and tinyurl link to a piccie doesn't do it.

Teens want rich social lives, not short messages. And the investment they made in building their MySpace page, which then had to be reinvested to build their Facebook page, just won't work in Twitter.

Twitter doesn't allow you to bling your profile y'see. Facebook does.

So this report is old news ... or news for oldies.

EU project to track all your tweets (2009)

One of the drawbacks of social media is their potential for breaches of privacy. For example, I stumbled across Wikileaks this week, a website that leaks all sensitive information into public domain such as the leak of the UK's Ministry of Defence document on how to stop leaks.

There's tons of fascinating stuff in there, and one of the more recent leaked documents is the European Commission's Working Package 4 (WP4) which aims to crawl all over your Facebook status updates and Twittering tweets to see if you're a terrorist or anarchist.

Here's the lowdown:

EU social network spy system brief, INDECT Work Package 4, October 4, 2009

> "This file, marked "confidential", describes development of an EU-funded intelligence gathering system ("INDECT work package 4") designed to comb web blogs, chat sites, news reports, and social-networking sites to in order to build up automatic dossiers on individuals, organisations and their relationships.
>
> "The aim of work package 4 (WP4) is the development of key technologies that facilitate the building of an intelligence gathering system by combining and extending the current state-of-the-art methods in Natural Language Processing (NLP). One of the goals of WP4 is to propose NLP and machine learning methods that learn relationships between people and organisations through websites and social networks ...
>
> "Given an XML data corpus extracted from forums and social networks related to specific threats (e.g. hooliganism, terrorism, vandalism, etc.); an annotation and knowledge representation scheme that should provide the following information:
>
> - The different entity types according to the requirements of the project;
> - The grouping of all references to an entity together;
> - The relationships between different entities;
> - The events in which entities participate."

There's nothing that surprising about this development. If anyone thought their Facebook and Twitters were private for example, then they are mad. As soon as you record anything electronically it's in public domain and all government authorities will track and analyse your thoughts, comments, status updates and more.

Bank's tweets and twitters (2009)

Interesting discussions going on about the latest social media craze, Twitter.

According to Twitter's website: "People are eager to connect with other people and Twitter makes that simple. Twitter asks one question, 'What are you doing?' Answers must be under 140 characters in length and can be sent via mobile texting, instant message, or the web."

I Twitter through various feeds as do around seven million other folks, and it is a great short message service for those who want to lifestream (social networking phraseology for sharing one's life digitally).

So Twitter is basically an easy way of linking your internet and mobile lifestyle with easy updates.

The site has been around since March 2006 and shot to fame in the last few days because the first photograph of the Hudson River US Airways crash was broadcast on Twitter, via a user's upload from their mobile phone.

I'm talking about it today because banks are vulnerable to identity theft issues via Twitter, just as they are via Facebook and other social media.

First, there are the obvious user issues with identity, e.g. I know what you did last summer and all that. More importantly however, is the ability to use Twitter to steal a bank's identity.

Right now, I can point to a few banks that are using Twitter to improve customer communications, such as Wachovia and

Bank of America, along with a few social finance sites such as SmartyPig.

But most banks are not twittering yet and, for this vast majority, they should own their Twitter name at the very least or it might get hijacked. Some banks have secured their name, such as Wells Fargo (isn't that Wachovia?) which is holding the Wells Fargo Twitter name just in case. Some may or may not be secure, such as Citi and their variations Citigoup and Citibank.

Whilst a few are obviously fake, such as JPMorgan's and Nat_West (which a friend of mine set up whilst we watched a football match).

What this means is that banks must be careful about Twitter as it could be as easy to undermine a bank's brand here as the old days of the internet Wild West, when folks used to register domain names in the hope of multimillion dollar payouts by firms to get them back.

Wouldn't you feel like a bunch of tweets if that happened?

Insider trading and Twitter (2009)

I wondered recently about the potential of market abuse in new social media. This was inspired by an April Fool from the *Insurance Post,* which had the headline: "FSA proposes ban on social networking sites".

This was a joke but I have a growing feeling that Twitter is a great medium for generating market abuse through insider trading.

For example, using a duff email address – it's easy enough to get one on AOL or Yahoo! – you could create your Twitter pseudonyms and then merrily exchange insider news and views completely out of the loop of the regulator's eye. I just created one a minute ago, for a laugh.

Now ok, this could just be me mucking around but how would they know? And if they did find abuse and wanted to track me down, how would they do it? Through my IP address?

You see, even if the regulator could track down exchanges, could they track those Twitters back to me if I were using a pay-as-you-go mobile or Blackberry?

No ID, no address, no nothing. Just a thought.

200 million users today (2009)

A website created in 2004 reached 200 million users on 8 April 2009. That's the size of America near enough! A website has built an America in just five years.

Not bad going is it, and, even though it's not a bank, this is as important to banking as the internet as it has become the home page for almost 200 million people.

The site is Facebook, as if you didn't know, and here's Mark Zuckenberg's note explaining what it means to them (a lot of share options I would have thought):

> "We will welcome our 200 millionth user to Facebook some time today, and I want to take this opportunity to describe what this means to us and what we hope it can mean for everyone using Facebook.
>
> "When we built Facebook in 2004, our goal was to create a richer, faster way for people to share information about what was happening around them. We thought that giving people better tools to communicate would help them better understand the world, which would then give them even greater power to change the world.
>
> "Creating channels between people who want to work together towards change has always been one of the ways that social movements push the world forward and make it better. Both US President Barack Obama and French President

Nicholas Sarkozy have used Facebook as a way to organise their supporters. From the protests against the Colombian FARC, a 40-year old terrorist organisation, to fighting oppressive, fringe groups in India, people use Facebook as a platform to build connections and organise action.

"More broadly, technology has made it easier and faster for people across the world to share more and more – from the daily activities of their lives to events that impact their communities. At Facebook, we want to build the best service in the world for people to connect with and share everything that is important to them, whether day-to-day or world-changing. A heat map of our growth since 2004 shows how quickly people across the world are connecting on Facebook.

"Growing rapidly to 200 million users is a really good start, but we've always known that in order for Facebook to help people represent everything that is happening in their world, everyone needs to have a voice. This is why we are working hard to build a service that everyone, everywhere can use, whether they are a person, a company, a president or an organisation working for change.

"To celebrate and support all of these voices and their potential to improve the world, we are creating a space on Facebook where people can share their stories about how Facebook has helped them give back to their communities, effect change or connect with a distant relative. We've also worked with 16 charitable and advocacy organisations to create gifts that are now available in our gift shop. The organisation the gift represents will receive between 90 percent to 95 percent of the cost of the gift, after administrative expenses for the transaction, so we encourage you to share your passion for a cause with your friends and in doing so, support the cause. Facebook will not keep any part of your contribution.

"There are still many more people and groups in the world whose voices we want to connect with everyone who wants to hear them. So even as we celebrate the 200 millionth person and all of you using Facebook today, we are working to bring the power of sharing to everyone in the world."

Using social networks in the workplace (2009)

Why do some companies get the future faster than others?

Social networks. For example, BT has 16,000 employees on Facebook whilst IBM has more.

Is this wasting their time and ours? No. Why? Because the company that has the most employees using Facebook is Goldman Sachs.

Goldman Sachs must have a reason for encouraging this. They have 22% of their workforce using Facebook to share knowledge (I've not been able to substantiate this number, by the way). There's something in that, and we should all consider the impact this is having on their business, organisation and competitiveness.

What a bunch of bloggers (2008)

It amazes me how many employees of banks are using Facebook to track their feelings and thoughts about their firms. Most are saying things about how they hate their bank (hundreds of groups of that sort) with one real example being "I work for X Bank". This Group has a few hundred members with forums and discussions of the type: "What's the best thing about working for this bank?" and answers such as: "The end of my shift". You get the picture.

So, the truth is that you cannot hide anything anymore and therefore you might want to encourage staff to blog. Most banks are hesitant because they feel they cannot control the conversations. Well, don't. You cannot control people's thoughts. You cannot control their conversations. You cannot ban people talking around the coffee machines and water coolers. So create a platform to hear it.

That's the point of today's world. Have a conversation and join in. Understand what people think and listen. Some banks do this, but most banks do not.

And for the banks that are hesitant but want to really know what is going on around this social media world, then I would recommend books such as 'Join the Conversation' by Joseph Jaffe, a consummate blogger from the marketing world. His book offers some really good insights into what happens when you create an online two-way interaction.

The bottom line is: join the conversation. If you do not, you will have ostracised yourself from the world of today.

Postnote: One of my colleagues was recently using Twitter during a panel discussion. His tweet stated that the moderator talked too much and various folks in the audience agreed on Twitter. This was a silent conversation during the real world conversation. Real-time streams from individuals is the world of 2008. So the next time you're in a meeting, see if anyone is Twittering. You never know, your every word may be reported on the internet in real time.

Bankers face the book due to Facebook (2007)

It amazes me that, after talking about City boys losing their jobs due to Facebook and identity thieves targeting Facebook users, so many bankers allow their personal details to be fully accessible to all and sundry. By way of example, I recently was looking for certain people on Facebook and found the following about one individual:

JM who is male, lives in London, married to Jane, 39 years old (and yes, I know his birthdate), has a mobile and email that is publicly available, was educated at the London School of Economics and City University, and has worked at Barclays Bank as a Manager of Credit Risk but is now Director of Finance and Administration at another finance house.

By the way JM, sorry for publishing all of this info but you put it out there on Facebook. In fact, I also know who your friends are, that you like Zizzi's restaurants and skiing, and that you are a pessimist. So you should be.

Now, I don't know JM and I've never met him, but I know how to use Facebook to see people's profiles ... even though I'm not connected to them. This is the fallacy that most people believe - that you can only see your profile if you are in my connected network of friends.

FALSE!

JM's details are just one of hundreds of returns from my search of people I don't know and who aren't in my friends list.

So I then thought, what if I wanted to find a bank teller who could be blackmailed into helping me with a branch robbery. Enter Facebook and I find a lovely young lady born on October 6th 1987, who is a bank teller. She likes Harry Potter and clubbing, but hates men (so what's new?). She supports cancer charities and has a best friend called Christi. She also has her mobile number and email address on her profile, so I telephone Ms. X, and arrange a meeting. And so on and so forth ... you get the idea.

What all of this should tell you is keep two Facebook profiles: a public one and a private one.

The public one should show everything you'd like a stranger to know about you. The private one should be totally anonymous because, as soon as you start connecting, I'll find you. And if I can find you, so can your employers, identity thieves, bank robbers, the government ... you name it.

Closebook.

Risk: business enabler or idea crusher? (2007)

Opening up banks to transparency of operations may sound revolutionary, but that's what banks will have to do as the market and the customer is demanding it. Regulatory change is creating transparency, as is technology.

Facebook, for example. The idea of employee blogs and Facebook for bank staff is a heresy. Imagine a bank CEO saying "Hello there, I want to allow all of our staff to make decisions, act like humans and blog and talk about it online." This is the stuff of fiction. Nevertheless, banks cannot stop this.

By way of example, here's an interesting Facebook group called "I work at f#@!in Commerce Bank!!!" with wonderful comments such as:

> "Is anyone else tired of coming to work each day and finding out that they changed the way we do something."
>
> "It's the most convenient bank for the customer, but sucks for the employees."
>
> "Friday is my last day at Commerce!! love my co-workers but as for the company i say good riddance!!"

The idea of being able to keep anything secret anymore is rubbish. For example, I heard just last week that one bank's complete internal operating policy on AML was posted on Facebook by one foolhardy employee.

As a result, banks will find they cannot control such information seepage but will need to start opening up to transparency and new ideas. Risk will morph to become a business creating function, a business enabling function, a business supporting function ... rather than an idea breaking function, an innovation crushing function, an entrepreneurial killing function.

Facebook testing virtual currency (2009)

Interesting note sent to me from Nelson Eduardo Pereira today, who spotted that Facebook is offering a currency. It's not a real one, just swapping credits, but it's a start.

The service builds on the gift services in Facebook. These gift services have been tracked by Lightspeed Ventures for a while now and estimated to be worth around $15 million a year back in January 2008, increasing to $35 million by September 2008 and probably upwards of $60 million today.

What it implies is that Facebook has launched a first phase, virtual currency for swapping appreciation in virtual units amongst their now almost 200 million users.

Tomorrow? Cashing in those credits for trading in real money?

Can't be far away ... oh yeah, that's Spare Change, isn't it?

Where is the PayPal for Facebook? (2009)

Most social media is targeted at a conversation, which creates an advisory and support service. Talking with customers through social media makes sense, but where's the PayPal for Facebook?

Surprisingly, there is very little monetary activity in Facebook.

Maybe that's because of excellent stand-alone social finance services, such as Mint, Wesabe, Social Picks and more, who have all made some inroads to integrating their capabilities with Facebook ... or maybe Facebook's insecurities scare away any financial activities.

Regardless, the only service to gain any traction so far appears to be Spare Change. Spare Change has 134,000 active monthly users. Compare that with Pay Me, which has only 77 active monthly users, and you can see that capitalising on this social stuff may be hard after all.

There a couple of other interesting financial applications on Facebook, such as:

- Money, a new application from Michael Moriarty that allows friends to send each cash;
- Chipin, which is useful for rasiing cash for parties; and
- MyMoney from Fiserv, which is designed for credit unions to play in this space.

But, overall, the majority of financial applications on Facebook are games.

This is why we could generally claim that Facebook is for socialising and not for secure payment processing. That does not preclude advice, which is what I keep pushing financial providers to consider through such sites, but monetary transactions? Maybe not.

How Facebook payments could work in the future (2010)

Imagine Facebook creates a partnership with a global bank – let's say HSBC – to offer a P2P payments service. Not Facebook credits, but proper P2P payments. How might it work?

Today, I found out. I got Hyves.

Yes, I know that sounds like some sort of disease but it's not. It's actually the Dutch version of Facebook, and is the largest social networking tool in the Netherlands, with almost two-thirds of the population connected (9 million users out of a population of around 16.7 million people).

On March 24th, Hyves announced the introduction of social payments in partnership with Rabobank, a Dutch bank and also one of Europe's most innovative retail banks.

Patrick de Laive, co-founder of Twittercounter and Paydro, explains how it works:

> "With Hyves Payments you can send and receive money via your Hyves account. To each profile a link 'send money to' is added and you can instantly transfer amounts up to 150 eur to any one in the network. You can connect your Hyves account to your bank account (any bank in the Netherlands will do) to add money to or withdraw money from your Hyves account.
>
> "Hyves users can also request money from their friends. Very useful after a night out.
>
> "All payments are debit payments for peer-to-peer transactions, no costs are involved.
>
> "At the same time Hyves Payments are open for merchants and because of a partnership with cash register system Eijsink, and mobile application MyOrder 30% of the restaurants and bars in the Netherlands instantly can accept Hyves Payments.
>
> "For Merchant payments a €0.15 fixed transaction fee is charged to the merchant.
>
> "This is a perfect example of how a true local social network can add value over the big international ones. I can't see Facebook integrating a free peer-to-peer payment system for all their users. For stuff like this, deep integration and strong local partners are required. In this case Rabobank has the bank license, takes care of the money transfers and they also have an MVNO (Mobile Virtual Network Operator) that handles the text messages involved to authenticate the

payment. On the merchant side a partnership with Eijsink and MyOrder."

Licuro – an eBay for savings (2009)

When Zopa launched, many referred to them as a kind of eBay for loans. When Bidroute launched, it described itself as an eBay for trading even though they appear to be no longer trading themselves.

Now there's another eBay in finance: Licuro. Licuro is an eBay for savings, and is based on the highly successful Scandinavian MyBanker system, which effectively allows people with money to place it onto their site where banks bid for having a slice of the action.

The way it works is that you register with Licuro and typically place £50,000 or more. It can be used for lesser amounts, but they advise that you only save for less than three months if saving under £50,000.

Once you've registered, which costs £5.75 , you place the amount, time and currency (mainly USD, GBP, EUR) you wish to offer.

The site also advises that if you do deposit USD, GBP, EUR, then you can benefit from highly-competitive time deposit rates offered by Scandinavian deposit takers.

Within two hours, financial firms who want that money place various interest rate bids against your funds. These competing bids come from banks and building societies registered by the Financial Services Authority.

For each bank offer received, "you can view the interest rate, the interest return, and information about which deposit taker has extended the offer. Furthermore, you can see how much time you have before the individual offers expire. You may then accept one or more of the offers", although you are under no obligation to accept any of the offers extended.

MyBanker has been running in Scandinavia since 2002 and really took off when access to capital became more difficult. Today, they claim to be processing more than £700 million per month.

Now then, who's gonna do that eBay for mortgages ...

YouTube if you want to ... (2009)

Whilst researching banks' use of social media, I searched for the YouTube channels offered by banks.

The World Bank has a channel. And Barclaycard is in there, as a sponsor. Bank of America has a channel, called 'Your Money' (only available in the US). Wells Fargo has one.

But it was difficult finding many others.

Can banks ever be cool? (2007)

It is interesting to look at all the stuff about social networking sites MySpace, YouTube, Facebook, Second Life, Zopa and so forth. As the momentum builds you wonder what traditional banks are doing. But I saw an interesting survey by marketing firm Edwards Groom Saunders which kinda makes the point about what's happening today.

The firm talked to adults aged between 16 and 54 about the media that most influences their purchasing habits. By way of example, when buying a new mobile phone, 30% of consumers mentioned online social networking sites as being most influential, which is more important than billboard posters (25%). Nevertheless, mainstream TV still wins, with three-quarters saying ITV advertising and just under half Channel 4 which are the UK's two traditional terrestrial commercial TV channels.

Happiness for those folks blowing major budgets on TV networks. Maybe not, because if you look underneath the numbers a little bit more then you find that 16- to 24- year olds have a totally different picture of their influences, with 63% saying YouTube and MySpace are their most important influences, way ahead of ITV (50%) and billboards (20%).

It's not even as easy as that, as firms need to consider how to integrate and access these services, and which are most important to their brand and customer demographic.

For example, Bebo is for kids, MySpace for general teens and 20-somethings, Facebook for young professionals, LinkedIn for general professionals, Second Life for 25- to 34- year old German and American men (the largest group of users) and so on.

The bottom line is that banks and other businesses are shotgun blasting holes in their marketing budgets, chucking cash at internet social networks without much of a clue as to where it's going or what the returns are.

For example, when I go Second Life and visit their virtual branches, I usually find that there's no-one there – not even any staff – and I wonder why they're doing this.

Equally, if I'm networking about the latest Chemical Bros gig at Glastonbury on MySpace or Facebook, do I really want to respond to an advert for an account with MegaBank Corp?

Maybe banks should stick to advertising in specific channels, such as a great magazine for kids called 'Oink!' Oink! is named after the piggy bank … no puns related to The Pigs of Capitalism (now there's a good name for a rock band).

The post-Facebook webolution: checking in (2010)

As usual, some good stuff in *Wired* magazine this month. One article stood out for me in particular, which is about the rivalry between Foursquare and Gowalla. I'd heard of Foursquare but not much about Gowalla, and now see the next rise of web usage in more clarity.

Both sites are about checking in with your mates and being able to track where they are, what they are doing and whether there's anything interesting happening nearby. Like seeing the GSM signals of all of your friends in real-time.

Sure, Google Latitude was a good start point for this stuff, but there's now many new ways of socialising this physical and virtual network. For example, you arrive in London and know that someone had recommended the Comedy Club ... but which one. There's quite a few in London and you might not get the one that was recommended.

But it goes further as these sites link mobile, social, gaming and location. Like a Facebook with rewards. The idea is to get badges for visiting locations, and awards for achievements. So, if your peer group think McGinty's Bar is cool, then you'll get an award if (a) you get to McGinty's and (b) you down a shot of whisky chaser at the rear bar. All of which can be tracked in real-time and checked by your friends through the geolocation services.

In other words, you set challenges and take challenges, and get badges on your social profile for achieving.

Great stuff.

What really stood out in the article though, is this chart from John Battelle, who co-founded *Wired US* and wrote "The Search: how Google and its rivals rewrote the rules of business and transformed our culture".

Fields in **The Database of Intentions** As of Early 2010 (v2)		
Field	**Signal**	**Current Players (sample)**
The Purchase	What I buy	Amazon, ebay, Walmart
The Query	What I want	Google, Yahoo, bing
The Social Graph	Who I am Who I know	Facebook, myspace, Google
The Status Update	What I'm doing What's happening	Twitter, Facebook, Google
The Check-in	Where I am	foursquare, yelp, Gowalfa

As you can see, the chart shows the five revolutions tracked through the connected network and could be reworded as:

1. Buying stuff
2. Finding stuff
3. Building a community
4. What are you doing?
5. Where are you doing it?

On that basis, I think I could speculate about a few more cycles of revolution to come:

1. Who are you doing it with?
2. How are you doing it?
3. Can I come too?

Or something like that anyways.

Chapter 4 Social finance

Introduction

The idea of social finance and social banking is a bit weird. Banking, finance and money is antisocial, so this ain't right. But that's where things are changing. Finance can be social. Just look at new services like SmartyPig, Zopa and PayPal and you find lots of socially-oriented aspects to finance, because finance and banking is not really about money. It's not even about payments. It's about the enabling of people and businesses to exchange value, to have fun, to gratify needs, to experience what they want and need. It's about life. And that's why social finance works. Banks and many traditional financial providers are yet to wake up to this, but they will. If they don't, then someone else will.

Social finance is right here, right now (2008)

We have previously discussed social media and social networks, and their relevance to banks. The conclusion is that banks cannot ignore these developments, and need to use these communication capabilities to engage their audience in a conversation that advises, supports and educates potential customers in their financial capabilities.

This advice, support and education can build into a relationship and a trust that might generate future account openings, but that is not the primary intention. The primary intention is to build trust. After all, banks have lost so much trust this year, this must be a strong reason for social networks and media to be used as a critical platform for future business.

Let's look at going beyond advice and trust and see what new business models are developing around these themes.

From a social networking view, the most popular developments are around investment networks, such as Seeking Alpha, Social Picks, and the re-energised Motley Fool.

These are social networks for bankers and day traders seeking investment tips, and serve an interesting function in aggregating the views of the populace. This can therefore provide tips for where to avoid (where they're investing) and where to invest (where they're not investing).

Above this level, the main areas of financial activities are focused around lending, saving, budgeting and managing money.

In the latter two categories, services such as Mint and Wesabe have staked a strong claim to fame.

These services allow you to create a structured analysis of your saving and spending habits, and they proactively analyse your habits to help you manage them better. They will alert you when you're breaking your deposit balance rules, such as having too much or too little cash in your account. Similarly, they will tell you where you can find a better deal and offers suited to your financial habits.

How they do this is very similar to Amazon. Just as Amazon compares your buying habits every time you buy a book, CD or game, in order to recommend other books, CDs and games, Mint and Wesabe analyse all the people like you and recommend financial products, services and firms that might suit you better, based upon your profile and the profile of people like you.

This leads to one of the best banking service I've seen, *Tu Cuentas* from BBVA. *Tu Cuentas* means 'You Count' in English, and provides Mint and Wesabe style functionality, but from a bank.

BBVA will compare your profile with all the other BBVA customers, in order to give you alerts and offers with great precision, but it goes a lot further than this through aggregation services, budgeting services, investment services and alerts. It allows you to access *Tu Cuentas* services using Blackberry, mobile and internet platforms. It even allows you to use bits of *Tu Cuentas* services as widgets, which you can pick up and drop into any other web applications. So I could drop my bank balance and alerts on my Google personalised home page.

Fantastic.

These are all social banking services focused upon better financial management using digitally socialised tools.

Then we have new business models, such as social lending. Social lending first appeared in March 2005, when the UK's Zopa service was launched. Since then, Zopa-style lending services have appeared everywhere, from Smava in Germany to ppdai in China. In fact, in these times of the credit crunch, where people can no longer get access to funds from banks, social lending has become indispensible.

The basic premise of social lending is to create an eBay style platform for savers and borrowers. The savers' savings fund the borrowers' borrowings, just like a bank, but the difference is that these businesses offer no financial management themselves. They are just a platform to connect savers who want a higher return on their savings, and borrowers who want a lower interest rate on their loans. These platforms just connect them and claim that there is no financial management taking place.

Zopa, Smava, ppdai and related firms are therefore like eBay. eBay makes nothing but just connects buyers and sellers and, in the same way, these firms purely connect savers and borrowers. This is why Zopa falls outside the remit of the FSA, although they are regulated now as a result of offering insurance on their loans.

They also win out because they are small and nimble, with few staff or overheads, which means that they can offer a service with minimal spread on the difference between borrowing and saving rates. As a result, they undercut bank rates significantly with a 0.5 percent spread.

This is why social lending works.

It is now without issues, however. For example, this is why the US government is trying to shut some of them down.

The problem with the service, as cited by the SEC, is that loans are not being repaid and this is the challenge for these sites: to get enough liquidity to be able to cover all the borrowings required, and to manage the risk of those borrowings.

Many of the social lending sites cover these risks by using Experian, Equifax and other credit rating agencies, or through the offer of insurances, but any squeeze on funding strains the social lending business model.

That is why there are other things happening of interest to add to the social lending concepts, such as SmartyPig. SmartyPig takes the social lending model and applies it to savings. The way it works is that you set up an account and create a savings goal, such as saving for a car or a college education or to pay off a mortgage. As you save towards your goals, you tell the world by placing the SmartyPig widget on your social network page, blog or website. Lo and behold, all your friends and family can contribute towards your savings goals.

This is very friendly and very family oriented. As a result, SmartyPig had customers in all 50 states within three months of launch in the US are now partnering with other banks, such as ANZ, to launch a white-labelled service in Australia.

And these social models are not restricted to just the retail markets, although I guess we would call them Web 2.0 applications in the investment markets as there's nothing social about those markets.

For example, in the investment and trading space, you could say that Europe's new stock exchanges – Chi-x, Turquoise, BATS et al – are social exchanges. After all, they are new exchanges trading at minimal spreads by using the latest internet technologies to offer trading platforms that have virtually zero overheads. It's not social, but it's very similar to the structures of Zopa and similar companies in concept.

There's even an eBay for traders out there today. It's called Bidroute.

There are many other examples of new social style financial and banking offers. I contend that the world of social banking is developing fast. There are many firms out there building social models for finance, ranging from social advice to social lending and saving to social trading and dealing.

Every aspect of social media and social networking can be applied effectively to banking models. The difference in this world is one golden rule.

You are offering a platform for lower cost banking and trading for those people who like to serve themselves by participating. They participate because they believe it offers better value and service.

These new models are not pushing a product to customers. They are offering a platform to participants.

This golden rule is probably the hardest lesson for a bank, and will mean that most will follow or acquire these new business models, rather than invent or create them.

That's my guess, anyway.

Why social finance, and particularly Zopa, matters (2009)

It's worth looking at the business models of the new entrants who are trying to disrupt this space and pose the question: are they sustainable?

Zopa, Prosper, SmartyPig, Wonga, Mint, Wesabe and the many other new entrants into finance hoping to leverage the promise of Web 2.0 technologies and social networks: can they last?

(...)

Are these new organisations serving new demands in new customer segments, in which case they are sustainable; or simply targeting the same traditional customer base as banks with just a social layer on top?

First, most of these new businesses are based upon a model of social connection first, with finance second.

This, to my mind, is the same as First Direct and PayPal, both of which are sustainable. First Direct was built upon a model of being a bank without branches built for the telephone channel. They were targeting the same customers as traditional banks but using a new channel for reach.

The core point of First Direct's model was: how could a bank operate without branches? This is why they are the best call centre bank in the UK, because they built a bank on a channel rather than a channel on a bank.

The target was the same traditional customer base as banks, with just a call centre on top.

And they are sustainable.

In First Direct's case they are owned by a bank and always have been, but the premise that a business is not sustainable just because it is targeting existing customers in a new way does not hold up.

For example, PayPal was targeting existing customers in a new way. PayPal's business is built upon payments by credit card or bank account but through a new channel – the internet. Their new way therefore was to offer secure online payments to traditional bank customers and that has been a phenomenal success, so much so that banks now say that they wish they had thought of the idea or bought PayPal before their success. They just didn't realise how successful and disruptive they would be until it was too late.

And this is a critical point: it's hard to get on a train once it has left the station.

At the core of the banker's argument therefore, which I refute, is that Zopa's strategy is flawed because they are targeting traditional customers of banks with just social media on top.

This is the reason why Zopa's strategy is fine, in fact.

If we get it the right way round: Zopa and their siblings have a lean and mean social networking machine at their core, and then target traditional customers of banks with razor-thin margin products and services that are fun, social and human. Their razor-thin margins are sustainable, unlike traditional banks, because they do not have the staff, legacy, bricks and mortar overheads and costs of traditional banks. And that would be my second point. They have no legacy overhead and are sustainable because their fixed cost structures are a fraction of the legacy competition.

This is why they matter and are disruptive.

Third, these new business structures are fledgling but they are taking off. Zopa has passed the £50 million of loans milestone and does 40% of that in just this year alone. Compared to the banks the numbers are of course tiny, but the pace of growth is quite remarkable.

The same is true of SmartyPig, a business that teams with banks. SmartyPig tell me that they currently have $170 million in core deposits in the US, and projections are to hit $500 million by year end. This is for a business that only launched in April 2008, and one that spends nothing on advertising.

How has SmartyPig achieved such phenomenal growth? A mixture of factors, from partnering with banks – West Bank in the USA and ANZ in Australia – but that factor is far less important than the fact that they get social media.

And this is the third point – these new business models are built for the 21st century consumer.

Take SmartyPig's business model. Zero advertising but a great blog, actively twittering, and easily widgetised into Facebook, MySpace or wherever you want to plug and play.

Here's a great example of their business model: the Twitter contest.

Each month they flag on their blog that they're going to be giving away $100 gift cards via a Twitter contest. The question is posed at a set time – let's say 8:00 pm. – and runs for 15 minutes from the tweet that asks the question. The first correct answer to the question posed wins.

All in all, a great use of the new media and an illustration of how this creates the multiplicity effect through the network buzz.

And SmartyPig are not alone in getting this: look at any other new entrant to finance on the web such as Mint, Wesabe, Zopa and more and they all have active blogging communities. This is because they get social media.

Fourth, as illustrated, these businesses are targeting new customers in a new way as well as existing customers. The fact that they are leveraging new 21st century technologies means that they will be reaching new 21st century customers. A little like First Direct saw the opportunity for call centres and PayPal for online secure payments, Zopa and their brethren envisage the opportunity for social media.

That's why the demographics of these businesses are so different. For example, Lloyds, is well-known in the UK as the bank that's full of old people who don't open new products. Lloyds has been continually challenged with reaching the under-35 age group – the group most likely to be the next generation of loyal customers as customers don't switch banks after the age of 35. And there's the missed opportunity. By thinking that Zopa and other social financial services are irrelevant, the banks miss the fact that they are securing the net generation of customers.

Can we prove this? I think so. Here's an insight into SmartyPig's demographics:

- 17% of SmartyPig's users are aged between 18 and 25;
- 40% are aged 26 to 35;

- 19% are aged 36 to 45; and
- 24% are aged 46 or older.

This shows the bulge bracket of new users is the core target base for next generation financial services; and the over 46 age group are their connections – the mums, dads and nans and granddads who invest and support the savings goals of their children and grandchildren.

That's a social network for you.

The average goal size of a SmartyPig saver is $15,000 over four years, with one out of five savings goals created on SmartyPig designated as 'public', so that everyone can see what I'm saving for.

And the top categories of savings goals are:

- 16% for travel;
- 14% for saving;
- 10% for an emergency fund;
- 8% for gifts and shopping;
- 7% for house deposit;
- 6% for home improvement;
- 6% for education;
- 5% for electronics;
- 5% for a car; and
- 8% for miscellaneous.

These are new business models of saving and connecting and, because these are new business models, we will see more and more hybrid versions of such businesses such as Caja Navarro's Zopa-style service.

Fifth, there's a view that banks can kill off these businesses once they prove any success. This view is a complete fallacy.

For example, taking another industry, the home shopping channel QVC was pitched as an idea to the major networks, but was seen as not being worthy of note until it gained critical mass.

What's critical mass, was the question posed. When you get 2.5 million viewers, was the answer.

The trouble is that when you get critical mass, you won't be interested in being acquired and selling out, because that's when the business is working.

Taking this and then adding the network effect, means that when Zopa starts working – let's say, it gets 2.5% of net new lending in 2011 – a year later, it can double, quadruple or even take 10 times that market share because, once it has reached critical mass, everyone will know what it is, what it can do and why it is relevant. That means they will trust it.

So, Zopa get 2.5% of net new lending in 2011 ... 2012 – 10%? 20%? Or more? This is highly likely and reasonable.

Then the banks think, let's kill it ... by undermining its pricing model? Zopa's pricing is razor-thin, so I don't think so. By buying it? Why would you want to sell out when you've just snatched victory? By copying it? Who has first mover advantage? Nope, as mentioned before, once the train has left the station, you can't get on it..

The real point is that, assuming there is a need for these new businesses, which I believe there is, the only thing that undermines their business model is access to ongoing capital to get to the point of success. This is the challenge of any new business, and this is the real challenge to these new entrants: can they fund the business long enough to be successful?

Luckily, there are plenty of financers out there who do believe in these new businesses to fund them through their fledgling beginnings, including Red McCoombs for SmartyPig; Zopa's investors range from Bessemer Venture Partners and Balderton Capital to the Rowland family.

Even so, in Zopa's case where they are creating a new market in P2P lending, the issue and challenge has always been getting enough people placing money into Zopa to enable them to meet the demands of those who want to borrow. Without funders, there is no marketplace.

So the challenge is to maintain investment and manage operating costs long enough during this start-up phase to get to the tipping point of growth. And, based upon a 40% increase in total loans just in the last year, maybe that tipping point has finally arrived.

However, it is critical to realise that, as with Friends Reunited and Lycos, the first generation of these services are not necessarily going to be the winners but, if we had seen the opportunity, would we not like to be a part-owner of Facebook and Google today?

Zopa – love it or loathe it? (2009)

I'm often asked about Zopa's business model and website Lovemoney have kindly made a video explaining what they're all about and how they work. At the end, they ask whether you should love or loathe Zopa ... you'll have to watch the video to find out the answer to that one.

Although the video is a bit naff, the comments area is interesting with MissingOz saying that: "Zopa is great, I've been using it for two years now ... Ironically, now I know how banks feel when faced with lending."

Oh to be a banker, and take real risks with your money.

And Max878 (what happened to the other 877 Max's?) says: "I'm a Zopa lender. Yes, it's a strong product. However, please bear in mind that the historical returns of over 8% are simply not realistically achievable. At the moment, you are not likely to be lending to A* borrowers at much over 7.5% if that. Zopa will take 1% of that in fees (not unreasonable bearing in mind that they carry out stringent checks on potential borrowers). Many lenders, myself included, believe that default rates are edging close to 1.5% - 2% at the moment, and it's not likely to improve in the near future. And you will of course be taxed on the interest that your investment earns."

It's not all fun and games in the world of borrowing and investing, is it?

Mind you, my favourite comment would have to be Olipro's, who reckons the presenter "talks in a tone that reminds me of the informational videos they show to children in school."

So, if Jack lends Jill one dollar and wants Jill to pay it back very quickly, Jack charges Jill more to borrow that dollar than he charges Mary ... but Mary is better looking, so that's why.

SmartyPig makes a Big Oink! (2009)

I'm always on the scout for new stuff in banking and SmartyPig is one of my favourite stories. A social saving service designed for social networks, they're a great little outfit and spoke at the Financial Services Club's American Retail Banker's forum I arranged last November.

Now, they're going from strength-to-strength with core deposits for West Bank, SmartyPig's banking partner, rising from about $10 million in February to more than $100 million now. Deposits should top $500 million by the end of the year, according to SmartyPig's co-founder Jon Gaskell.

Then, in the latest twist, SmartyPig have a billionaire benefactor in the form of Texan B. J. 'Red' McCoombs.

Why has Mr. McCoombs come on board?

Because "the technology that they have developed, and it's already proved itself, could handle 5,000 accounts or it could handle 5 million accounts", says Mr. McCoombs. "In essence, you can pay the customer more for the deposits because it doesn't cost you as much to process and manage them."

He goes on to emphasise that "they have produced the technology that is driving an opportunity the likes of which we seldom see."

SmartyPig is based in Des Moines, Iowa, US, with just 15 employees and describes itself as "an online savings tool that works with a bank to allow account holders to make their savings goals public."

Watch out, traditionalists. The march of social finance moves up a gear.

Mobile social money – the final frontier? (2008)

Mobile social money refers to the use of mobile devices as access media to these social networks, media and banking.

Mobile usage in banking has grown to a crescendo in 2008, after bubbling away nicely since the turn of this century. This is in part down to the fact that the latest smartphones allow a bank to deploy fully functional internet banking services to mobile devices using the same platform as their main websites. In other words, it is now cost-effective and appropriate to do this.

However, the challenge with mobile finance is that we tend to discuss mobiles as one homogenous group of devices when:

(a) There are many devices; and

(b) The use of mobile devices to access financial services are not homogeneous.

Let's look at (a) first.

This is important because the fully functional services, such as those from BBVA that allow mobile banking access using web browsers, are only available on smartphones. The first smartphones to offer full mobile web devices were not released until after 2004, and so this means that some users are unable to access the service.

Even if they can access, the challenge then is that there are many operating systems to choose from and handsets, and the services must be available and compatible with all of them. On the operating system side, you have BlackBerry, Windows Mobile, iPhone, Nokia's N Series, Symbian, Maemo (Linus), the Palm OS and more. Each of these systems provides different levels of internet access and usability, as do the handsets which also cover a multitude of providers and structures. Is your service designed for a flip phone (Motorola), a slide phone (Nokia N95), a rectangular phone (iPhone)? Is it for a phone with a full QWERTY keyboard, a touch-screen or both?

The devices can therefore seriously inhibit the usage of a service. Equally, some users may not be able to access the services at all if their phone is pre-2004. This is certainly true for many emerging economies and hence, when we discuss new payment systems such as M-Pesa in Kenya, the focus is on text messaging payments using SMS rather than mobile web-based banking services.

This leads on to point (b): there is a wide range of mobile financial services.

The basic service is the person-to-person (P2P) payments using SMS. This is how most remittance services work because the service is available on any telephone using GSM standards that date back to 1985. Therefore most senders and receivers will be able to use the payments service, regardless of the mobile device they use for access. This is also how PayPal Mobile started, although you can see from their website today that they also offer mobile web payments.

This leads to adding layers of financial services onto mobile access, which may include mobile billing presentment and payment (MBPP), account balances, alerts for payments or budgetary limits, and more.

The real point is to make it clear that mobile finance goes far further than just payments or a single class of financial activity. Today, it goes from everything from basic text message services to fully fledged banking services over the internet.

Equally, social money goes further than just the internet and may encompass anything from P2P payments between contactless devices, which are not necessarily mobile-based, and prepaid services on mobile, as well as gift cards.

In other words, social money is not just internet-based or mobile-based, but can be any form of transaction between individuals that enables people to exchange value directly and immediately between each other, as easily as a cash exchange.

Historically that has been a challenge, but now it is easy and can be anything from a mobile text message to the touch of a contactless card; from an email to a telephone call; and from a Linden dollar to a Totnes pound.

The FT picks up our social lending debate (2009)

The *Financial Times*' Money Matters blog has picked up on the debate between James Gardner and me about Zopa. They've asked readers for comments. I thought I would re-post some of the responses here as it adds to the richness of the context of our discussion.

Martin Campbell (the one that started this off) responds:

> "Certainly wasn't expecting it to all kick off as it has, but of course there is only one thing worse than being talked about...

"Can I just take the opportunity to correct a fundamental misunderstanding that has plagued much of the debate across these various blogs. Zopa is not a lender like a bank is. It is a MARKETPLACE. It is a radically different proposition from the banks.

"Zopa does NOT set the rates. Lenders make offers at the rates that they choose themselves. If borrowers think the rate is a good deal, they will take it up. If they don't, they won't and lenders will feel pressure to lower the rates they are offering to a level that borrowers will accept.

"So all this toot about 'price wars' and killing off Zopa when it becomes big enough is born of a lack of understanding of how the Zopa model works.

"If the banks wanted to kill off Zopa with a price war as James G says they will, they would kill themselves off first; the extent to which they would have to reduce their current rates is too big, the overheads they have to cover are gargantuan compared to Zopa's wafer thin operational costs (and charges) and because they would have to offer these new hugely loss-making rates to the whole country.

"They would be dead long before Zopa would be.

"Also, in response to an earlier comment, Zopa carries out all the credit and affordability checks that the banks do – and more.

"Far from being denied the information banks have, Zopa obtains far more than most do, and takes more factors into account, even a would-be borrower's eBay rating. Zopa also aims at a higher standard of "responsible lending" than most banks do – partly because it is not its own money that is being lent. The proof that they have got this right is a default rate that has never been higher than 0.5% – radically lower than the banks achieve."

GG says:

"Zopa provides great rates for lenders and borrowers but, for me, it's the satisfaction of beating the bankers at their own game that makes it great.

"Of course, there is no government guarantee and that is why I focus on the lowest risk markets. At the moment, returns are double those of the best cash ISAs."

Vinay Basavaraj states:

"I am sceptical of the role Zopa, and similar potential replacements, will play in the future. One fact that clearly undermines Zopa is the information advantage that banks possess. By means of the payment system, banks have acquired invaluable information of potential borrowers. What remains to be seen is whether this information advantage is eroded by an 'efficient market.'"

Othermotte says:

"I am a Zopa user and very pleased with it. I had money that I wanted to earn interest on and the only place to offer a decent return was Zopa.

"The fact that it was 'social lending' was an added incentive. In the past, I have had money in a number of mutuals and always voted against demutualisation, despite the bribe of shares that was offered. I think that the demise of building societies was a bad thing and Zopa offers something closer to that model. I actually enjoy browsing the comments from the myriad of borrowers and the connection that it makes to real people.

"But the bottom line is that it is a good interest rate for savers."

(...)

Comptroller adds:

"Zopa is, after four-plus years, very small, has operating deficiencies and obviously not fulfilling its initial business objectives (operating losses of £1million on a turnover of £673,000, reduction of staff literally in half from 2007 to 2008.) Activity spiked in early 2009 and has continued with steady growth but has nothing like the momentum required to threaten the banks.

"Despite recent publicity on national radio and in the press its activity is still less than the average branch of a high street bank (and about the same number of staff.) The rates of return are not bad but there is the risk of bad debt, and many lenders think this risk was inadequately flagged when they joined. Anomalies with tax and the better returns available elsewhere for about the same risk limit growth for the moment.

"In time Zopa will probably gain some critical mass if its backers are prepared to be patient and continue to support it, but it is unlikely that it will challenge the banks any time soon from its current position of less than 0.1% of the unsecured lending market in the UK."

GRR counters:

"As a lender in the current market conditions, Zopa offers a far superior return to even the best deposit accounts / fixed rate bonds, even after taking account of the notional cost of bad debts. However, you can't predict what will happen with your particular borrowers, and you have to accept the fact that, statistically speaking, it's possible that all your borrowers could default! But to say that the risk isn't evident to lenders is totally unfair – all the rates quoted make allowance for bad debts, there is ample guidance (and FAQs, etc), and the very nature of the model (multiple small-denomination loans to multiple individuals in predetermined credit bands) allows lenders to minimise their risk of exposure to unacceptable levels of risk of default.

"Add to this the feeling of doing something socially responsible, and a really well-thought-out and user-friendly interface, and Zopa is a winning proposition – just awaiting the critical mass which it needs to really take off and challenge the incompetent and immoral institutional lenders."

Colin Henderson throws in:

"The rates will be set by the market based on supply and demand. This is not the core of the argument however. The debate turns on business model characteristics.

"Banks are entering a productivity crisis. Their opportunities for revenue growth during a period of consumer retrenchment and deleveraging are low. That is why banks are looking at exiting large numbers of branches. However, they have not laid the groundwork by automation of the customer processes needed to support less branches. Automation has been focused on data management and not customer interaction.

"Zopa is built as an efficient platform and has begun to automate customer processes such as identity verification, and integration of credit scoring with lending processes in ways banks have not.

"The coming crisis of productivity will define losers and winners in this debate."

Toontopo pipes in with:

"I am absolutely convinced that Zopa and similar platforms will become an ever more important competition to banks. Personally I don't think of Zopa as the banking equivalent to e-bay, because unlike with e-bay, there is no one-to-one relationship between lender (seller) and borrower (purchaser).

Rather I like to think of Zopa as a facility that simply takes the potential of internet banking to the next level. Even if occasionally banks may still make better offers to potential investors or borrowers, in the long run they simply cannot undercut the substantial advantage that Zopa has in terms of overheads, an advantage that is entirely down to the potential inherent in internet."

Richardo27 adds:

"As Bill Gates reportedly said, "the world needs banking but it doesn't need banks". The way out of the financial crisis is not to prop up existing banks at all costs but to ensure banking services are available. This is where Zopa comes in and recreates the social benefit of banking, namely the availability of credit and the rewards attached to saving, both of which encourage long-term planning in individuals, without sucking up all profit for the middlemen. It is a new form of mutualism. This is such an attractive proposition for both borrowers and investors that it seems inevitable that it will grow much more important than it is now. Plus, it has a number of independent comparative advantages – entirely internet-based, absence of legacy bad debt, not at the mercy of wholesale markets – that can only further strengthen the model."

How a bank should respond to 'disruption' (2009)

The word 'disruptive' is being bandied about liberally in the debate about new competitors, such as Zopa.

First, as I've said before, banks don't really have any competition except between the incumbents, due to the structure of the industry. Second, where there are openings, then disruptive new players may find a way to find a niche which is what Zopa and their brethren are trying to do.

So what exactly is 'disruptive'?

Well, the term 'disruptive' in the management school sense, was coined by Clayton Christensen, the Harvard Business School Professor who wrote the book 'The Innovator's Dilemma'. I've seen Mr. Christensen present this concept a couple of times, and he talks about two types of innovation: sustaining and disruptive.

Sustaining innovation targets the existing market, whilst disruptive innovation either creates new markets or takes root with the incumbent's worst customers.

And a disruptive innovation cycle goes something like this ...

An industry grows up around a product or service. Over time, many companies enter the market and compete. Gradually, the competition moves from being the basic product to being the best product for a target market segment. As a result, lots of different market niches emerge, and competitors compete on building more and more functionality to appeal to their target markets. This leads to inefficiencies as the competitors add a lot of form and function that no-one needs but they have to add this as, otherwise, there is no desire to replace and repurchase. The industry over time becomes one where a lot of the price of the goods is going into form and function that the customer does not require, and so new competition comes in and disrupts the incumbents who are now too blind to see the folly of their ways.

The new competition enters with a new technology or approach. This new angle allows them to build the same product, but often stripped to the bones into the original basic and functional product and at a fraction of the price of the incumbents. The new competitor wins eventually, because the incumbents laugh it off when they first see it. The incumbents dismiss the new competition as being trivial. They pour scorn on it, as it is a no-frills basic service compared to their beautiful, functionally-rich offer.

The real issue though, is that the incumbents dismiss it as trivial but the market – the customer – does not. The customer wants it because it is cheap and simple, rather than expensive and complex. They want it because they are paying for what they get, rather than the irrelevant form and function the incumbents have added on top that they do not need.

By the time the incumbents realise this, it is when the new competitor is succeeding. By the time the new entrant is succeeding, it is because they have reached critical mass (above 2.5% of market share, according to some). By the time they have critical mass, the industry has disrupted and it is too late to turn things around for the incumbents, who are stuck with legacy structures and products.

And so the industry reignites and rebuilds in a new business model, having been disrupted by a new competitor using new technology to build a new way of doing business.

(...)

You could take this story and apply it to any industry. Think British Airways vs Virgin or Easyjet; AT&T vs Verizon; WHSmith and Barnes & Noble vs Amazon; Thomas Cook vs Expedia; and so on.

Or banks vs social finance, lenders vs social lending, and Lloyds and their cartel vs Zopa and their brethren.

Zopa's big attraction is that they purely provide a platform for people to sell money to those who want to buy money. Zopa sets no rates and makes their margin on the difference between the buy and sell rates, a few basis points of margin in other words.

The point I should underscore here, by the way, is that it is not that social lenders are necessarily cheaper as product, in the sense of the car illustration, but that they are cheaper as an operation. Because they operate at razor-thin margins, they give all of that margin that banks would take – the 1%+ differential – and give it directly to the customer.

That is their secret – not cheapness, but sub-1% margin operations.

The result is that Zopa and their brethren are disruptive innovators, gaining bank's customers who seek to borrow money at discounted rates from people who have money based upon basis point differential, rather than percentage point.

Equally, as banks currently offer really bad rates for lending and saving, they've already risen above being off-radar as they are taking at least 1% market share, and possibly 2%. This is because, as I've been telling all my mates who have bank savings accounts earning sub-4% interest, they could get 6% or more return on their savings through Zopa.

Is the risk greater with Zopa? No. They use the same risk management systems (Experian and Equifax) as the banks.

What if people don't pay me back? If you're worried about that, they offer an insurance policy you can buy for a small premium to cover your investment.

As a result, Zopa's funders and borrowers who are giving and taking money (liquidity) on their platform are building and, since this crisis hit, building more and more rapidly. This is because savers and borrowers can see that they can get better rates here than they can find anywhere else. Slowly, this will attract more money and, over time it may attract a lot more.

Once the banks notice the loss of their loan book, it is too late. The new operations will have critical mass and once you see critical mass, the train has left the station. So you can't get on the train – it's left – and if the new competition operates at margins of around 0.5%, then a bank cannot compete. Reason: how can a bank with thousands of branches, staff and fixed cost, suddenly operate at zero margin?

Add on to this the social, human and fun bit, and you can see where this goes, in terms of really innovative disruption. Now, right now, banks laugh at this new competitor because it is an irrelevant bit of fluff on their shoulder, a flea on their backside, a noise that cannot be heard.

After all, Zopa is purely attracting muckrakers buying rust buckets. Or maybe they are not. And maybe it's not them anyway. Maybe it will be Prosper, Boober, Smava, PPDai, SmartyPig, Wonga or one of the many, many others out there.

So a bank should compete. But how? Do what Caja Navarro has done, and create a hybrid social lending model that is bank run but the exchange of monies is between mums and sons, dads and daughters, aunts and cousins, friends and strangers.

Why should a bank compete? Not because it will make the bank money in the short term, as the margins are rubbish, but it will keep the bank in the food chain and stem the tide of any demand that disappears to a new fledgling before the fledgling finds its feet.

That's the real answer to this innovator's dilemma.

After all, if you just laugh at the flea on your backside, before too long you find the nasty little parasite has sucked all the blood out of you and ... you die.

In love with Kiva (2009)

For those of you who haven't heard of Kiva, it's a P2P lending community with a difference. It's the Grameen Bank of the Zopa world. In other words, it facilitates microfinance, using the web as an enabler. And it's wonderful.

Why is it wonderful? It starts with that fact that it connects people with money to those without.

I joined Kiva a while ago and put $100 in, just to see what happened. The investment was split into $25 chunks across four borrowers in four countries. Since then, I've been recycling the

$100 amongst different communities. On a regular basis, Kiva updates me with the progress of the loans made. The point is to help people out of poverty. Using the concepts of microfinance created by Muhammad Yunus, who received the Nobel Peace Prize for creating Grameen Bank, Kiva has taken this concept into the 21st century.

The organisation runs a network based in the US, with local agents managing the distribution and collection of money. As a result, there's a human connectivity here, which is why most loans are repaid fast.

The nice thing about Kiva is that it's social too. You not only feel connected to your remote investment, but also with the other investors.

All in all, it's a brilliant concept run by fantastic people and improves the world. And there's not many financial services companies you can say that about these days is there?

And there's another reason Kiva is important for you to be aware of. They're now moving into the mainstream. Early in June for example, they started microfinance for ... Americans.

I took particular note of the outcome of their move into micro-lending in the US:

"The Kiva Board had a lot of questions given the significant amount of both criticism and support of the US pilot from the Kiva lender community. After a lengthy discussion, we've decided three things:

1. Based on overwhelming feedback that Kiva is about giving people choice, Kiva should continue to give our members the choice to make loans to US entrepreneurs.

2. We've received tons of feedback regarding the perceived poverty level of certain borrowers who were part of the US launch. Kiva intends to sit down with our US-based field partners and share this feedback so that they can post loans that align more closely with Kiva's poverty alleviating mission.

3. As we consider future opportunities to expand within the US, we will exercise caution and keep the ongoing feedback of the Kiva lender community in mind."

Funnily enough, this reflects the fact that the Kiva community like the idea of helping Cambodia, Uganda, Nigeria and other under-developed economies, but many don't like the idea of people with money giving to economies where people have money ... the US, in other words.

The trouble is, these days, many in developed economies also need money and so Kiva has said that if Americans want to give to Americans, so be it. I wonder if they'll give to Glaswegians, as Muhammad Yunus thinks that's a good target?

A Spanish first: social banking (2009)

There are a few countries / continents where innovation is rife. In Africa, mobile payments are transforming the continent. In Japan, mobile internet banking is changing their world. And in Spain, social finance is top of the agenda.

Last year, I noted that BBVA had launched the first Web 2.0 banking application *Tu Cuentas* (You Count). Now Caja Navarra (CAN) have launched the first bank-led social lending system.

What this demonstrates is innovative thinking about the challenges of social lending sites like Zopa and Prosper. Rather than ignoring these new business models, CAN have created a hybrid where the bank provides a secure social lending platform and manages the relationships between those who fund and those who need funds.

Brilliant.

Oh yes, and in case you're asking, why would customers trust a bank to manage their social lending? In CAN's case – easy. They are not a bank but a civic bank. In fact, they are 'pioneers in civic banking'. They exist as a savings bank in the interests of their members and community, a bit like a community banks in the US or mutuals in the UK or Sparkassen in Germany. In other words, they are very member- and customer-oriented. For example, CAN give 30% of their resources to charitable and community based projects. That's why they are trusted to do this more than their larger, proprietary competitors.

Brilliant.

Wonga: another web disruption for loans (2009)

During the week, I enjoyed lunch with a venture capitalist who works with start-up firms that are innovating in financial services. One of the businesses he's investing in is Wonga, another business that appears to be disrupting banks' business models in the same way as Zopa has been.

I'd never heard of Wonga before, except in the colloquial English context where it means 'money', so my interest was immediately piqued. Googling the word when I got home, sure enough the first hit was their homepage, Wonga.com.

How imaginative!

I also then noticed that they appeared at FinovateStartup last year along with Mint, Prosper, Loanio and Wesabe, so they've been in good company (unfortunately, the presentation was confidential so it's not available on Finovate's website).

So what exactly do Wonga do?

Loans. They provide short-term loans though a 100% online process, with the funds typically transferred to your bank account within an hour. It's that last bit that's key and their elevator pitch: "we process loans without paper, totally electronically and immediately".

They need your name, address, marital status and employment details to do credit checks of course. Once clear, they send you a confirmation email and a unique PIN to your mobile. Then all you do is link back to the website to finish the application. This bit requires your debit card and bank details, the former for repayment on the date you set and the bank details to deposit the loan.

On first application, you're limited to £200 ($300) and, assuming you prove you're trustworthy, that can be increased over time. The loan is for a maximum of 30 days and no more, so it's not a credit service but a 'tide-me-over' service.

Mind you, with a £5:50 ($10) transmission fee and an interest rate of 1% per day (that's an APR of 2,334%!), you wouldn't want to keep the money for long. In fact, the cost of a one-month loan, including fees, works out to be 36.7%, so it's not advisable to keep money on Wonga for too long.

Even with all this, they're pretty popular. According to the *Guardian*, one of the few newspapers to have reported on the firm, Chief Executive Errol Damelin (a former investment banker) says that they "served over 50,000 customers during our testing phase and expect to help many more over the next 12 months." In particular, Errol makes it 100% clear that this is not microfinance, but commercial lending. At those rates he's right, although he does point out that it's good value for money if you're looking at these rates compared to bank interest rates and fees on overdrafts.

They've also made the *Red Herring* lists for the Top 100 European technology companies and Top 200 worldwide.

I can't say I'm surprised at this, as their whole business is completely automated with no humans involved in Wonga loans at all. That's why they only have 37 staff in London, with the rest of the development team in the Ukraine.

Worraloadofwonga!

Chapter 5 Social money and virtual worlds

Introduction

In 2006, everyone started to talk about Second Life. The reason was because *Business Week* had a front cover with the headline: "Virtual World, Real Money", and the sub-line: "She's fictional, lives inside an online game, but earns thousands of actual dollars there. And she's not alone." The story was about a German-Chinese lady, Anshe Chung, and how she was making over a million dollars in real life from selling virtual properties. The hype then began and before you knew it, everyone was using Second Life. The following year, Second Life failed because the banks failed. The lesson learned was that banks need to be licensed and regulated. In fact, in the virtual economy almost everything reflects the real economy. Therefore, as a bank, there should be a major focus upon these developments of commerce and trading. This is particularly true as there are now hundreds of virtual worlds out there, including many that are successfully creating virtual trade communities for online and offline commerce.

Social money – what's all that about then? (2008)

In this penultimate part of looking at how the internet world is creating new models of banking and finance, we'll look at social money, currency, cash or whatever you'd like to call it.

Before I do however, I forgot to mention one of my favourite examples of social finance, BillMonk, which keeps track of who owes who money in social networks. Sure, I know that all of you bankers out there won't need this type of service, as you manage this professionally, but I remember my student days and opening the fridge screaming: "Who's used my milk? Who's used my milk?"

It was darned annoying keeping track of the nickels and dimes we were all lending and borrowing from each other, and so a nice application that does this online is great.

Anyway, back to social money. Social money is the transfer of money electronically through any social media (blog, podcast, video) or network (Facebook, MySpace, Second Life, etc). Social money applications are all about buying games and emoticons, getting tips on blogs and charity fundraising. Anything where your social world needs a payment.

It has been around for years as an electronic IOU with the largest provider of social money being PayPal, although there are many other social money providers. Who remembers Beenz for example, and today there is everything from Web Money Transfer to c-Gold, from moneybookers to Ecocard.

The list is long, although the best known and trusted are from the largest online providers such as PayPal, Amazon and Google. These providers can be plugged in as widgets to almost any social media or social network, and hence are the real fuel for social money applications. For example, there are new developments in social money, such as Facebook's Pay Me and Spare Change, powered by PayPal.

It is not just limited to PayPal and internet money transfers as mobile money is also key. Social money also takes us into the realms of new money, such as Second Life's Linden dollars. Everyone talks about Second Life being a lot less popular today than it used to be, but it is worth explaining why that is.

Second Life's popularity disappeared when although their banking system collapsed in summer 2007. The banking collapse was a reaction to Second Life being forced to close down gambling facilities in their virtual world in July 2007. Until then, the website had been a phenomenon, growing from virtually no users to over 10 million in a year. This was incredible, and everyone felt it demonstrated the new emergence of business models.

In particular, the fact that Second Life allowed real commerce to be transacted by converting real US dollars to virtual dollars, meant that everyone started to test commerce in virtual worlds through the service. For example, several banks invested in major projects in Second Life, including ING, Wells Fargo, Saxo Bank and Deutsche Bank.

However, several banks also operated in Second Life that were managed by guys in their bedrooms. These included banks such as Ginko Bank, run by a Brazilian chap at home. The trouble Ginko Bank experienced started when internet gambling was forced to close under US laws. The management of Second Life decided that they also had to close access to gambling in virtual worlds in July 2007 to comply with this policy, which led to a major run on the virtual banks.

Until this date, a lot of the commercial transactions taking place in Second Life, where people converted real US dollars to Linden dollars, were for gambling purposes apparently. Therefore, the closure of gambling denizens in the virtual world meant that folks immediately started to take money out of the virtual banks – a bit like Northern Rock, but worse.

So imagine you are Andre Sanchez in Sao Paulo, the one-man band behind the virtual Ginko Bank. You have over a million real US dollars on account, translated into around 275 million Linden dollars that you are managing for the Second Life community.

Suddenly, your customers demand their money be converted back to real dollars, and you drown in their demands so you just close down the virtual bank, leaving punters with losses of around $750,000 in real life.

This led to calls for compensation from Linden Labs, which operates Second Life, but it said it wasn't its job to regulate the banks.

Oh dear.

Result: Second Life's popularity collapsed and, in a desperate move to rebuild trust, they said that only real-life banks with real world banking licences can now operate virtual banks.

Talk about virtual life mirroring real life ... mind you, I do note that Linden Labs didn't come up with a million dollar bail-out fund, so maybe not.

This is one example of social money systems and how they can reflect real world systems virtually. There's also the wonderful world of QQ in China, where currencies can be used for gambling and other illegal activities without governmental control.

These are just a few of the trends taking place in these new worlds, and we must not forget that there are many other areas we could talk around, particularly social money in the games worlds such as WOW (World of Warcraft).

These virtual and gaming worlds are fertile grounds for potential money laundering and fraud. By way of example, a fascinating report on virtual fraud was released by ENISA, the European Network and Information Security Agency, last week.

The report identifies that almost a third of gaming and virtual world users experience some form of fraudulent activity. With over a billion players spending over €1.5 billion in real money a year, there are some real issues here. For example, in just the last year, over 30,000 new malicious programs have been found targeting accounts and property in online games and virtual worlds, an increase of over 145%. Therefore, we do need to watch virtual and gaming worlds carefully, as they often reflect and even predict the issues we will be facing in the real world.

Before I finish talking about social money, it's also worth a quick doff of the virtual cap to complementary currencies. These currencies are on the rise as social money in the real world, and fuelled for broader acceptability through our networked world. For example, if I can exchange a London pound for a New York dollar of community effort via a trusted processor, then we could build a new, global complementary currency exchange.

This is the idea behind the Terra, a complementary currency promoted by the leading exponent of this area Bernard Lietaer. The Terra aims to be a social money, a complementary currency, that would provide a global exchange for trade, managed through internet technologies.

The problem with this currency is trust. Until a banking system operates such currencies they are hard to kick-start, which is why the Terra has been around for a few years in concept, but needs help to get started in practice.

In summary, social money is all about enabling the exchange of value between individuals and businesses through electronic channels.

This exchange can be:

- Formal, through electronic money transfer systems such as PayPal or exchanges based upon backing from valuable metals such as Gold and Silver; or
- Informal through exchanging real money into other forms of value, including virtual money and complementary currencies.

All of these are internet-fuelled and managed, to support the wider sphere of social finance, networking and media.

Layered upon these we then come to social money and finance accessed through other devices, where mobile money comes to the fore.

Zombie money in a chainsaw hell (2009)

I recently discovered that friends were killing me. Literally ripping me to shreds with a chainsaw. And it hurt. After all, I am meant to be the Zombie Priest in the Church of Goth, and no-one had beaten me before. And where did that chainsaw come from?

I was mad. In fact, I was steaming. So I vowed to get a chainsaw myself. Problem is that I would have to turn at least 40 friends into Zombies too in order to earn enough points to buy a chainsaw. And so far, I had invited over 200 mates to become Zombies and only 12 had bothered to do so. How would I get 40 of them to turn?

It was a problem. And I was still mad. In fact, I was boiling.

Then I found Spare Change. Spare Change sits on top of PayPal (which sits on top of the banking system) and, for a small fee for each transaction, allows me to make micro-transactions and buy things to spice up my favourite Facebook apps.

Oh, thank heavens for Spare Change. For just $5, I could buy a chainsaw. So I spent $50 and bought two chainsaws, plus a machete, shotgun, uzi, meat cleaver and bazooka for good measure.

Forget turning mates into Zombies ... just kill them. Now, I am the Zombie Pope in the Cathedral of Death. And Richard, the idiot who attacked me with a chainsaw, is dead meat.

Now you may wonder what the hell I am talking about, but the above is a real incident that occurred on Facebook last year, after I signed up for the game promotion of Resident Evil.

And Spare Change is a simple little Facebook app that allows me to buy things in Facebook gameworlds.

And these gameworlds are growing into big business. According to current estimates, the worldwide market for virtual goods is expected to approach $5 billion this year. That's $5 billion worth of exchanging stuff that doesn't exist ... but it's fun.

And it's also incredibly quick to build a business. For example, within a week of its launch, game company Zynga's new Café World game in Facebook had garnered 10 million players. Farmville, another game from Zynga that started this summer, already has over 60 million monthly users. And analysts reckon that about a tenth of these players buy stuff so, if a tenth of Zynga's 60 million farm players buy a cow or tractor for $5 this month, then Zynga are banking $3 million a month.

That is why another social game developer, Playfish, was acquired by the more traditional computer games developer, EA Games, for $275 million in cash last week.

This is big stuff.

Even bigger is the idea of using virtual worlds and social gaming to bling your profile.

That's how China's QQ coins started and soon became a phenomenon. Today, QQ international boasts over a billion users and more than 500 million active monthly users. That's four times the number of users of Facebook and six times more active users than PayPal!

These experiences indicate that the future of money is not money itself. We do not wake up and think about making payments and buying money, we think about waking up and thinking I'm going to use my money to buy something. So money is purely there for the value exchange. And if that value exchange can be achieved by using virtual coins, fantastic.

Conclusion: expect the world of the next decade to morph into a myriad of payment mechanisms that supplement, supplant and supply fun and games on top of the traditional banking network.

Oh yes, and expect billions of micro-transactions to occur person-to-person globally.

Second Life: I'm not dead yet! (2009)

According to some media Second Life is deader than the dodo, with the *Daily Telegraph* publishing its death knell last week.

"Research for The Daily Telegraph shows just 580,000 people logged on to the game last week."

Actually, that research was just some journo going to the Second Life's openly published stats and facts, and seeing that 589,147 residents logged-in during the last seven days. The article goes on to cite many business people who think it no longer has the legs to survive past the end of 2009.

I can see why folks may think Second Life has had it, but they would be wrong. For example, the numbers of logged-on residents during the last 60 days is 1,422,527 which is the same as the last time I looked in January 2008.

When, over a year later, the same numbers hold up then the community has stabilised and it is a great system for trialling virtual work and commerce.

The problem Second Life experienced, however, was that they let their banking system fail and disclaimed responsibility for it. (…) The virtual world operates in a very similar manner to the real world. The regulators of the virtual world, Linden Labs, abrogated their responsibilities when Ginko Bank failed which lost confidence. Equally, the US ban on gambling on the internet made it clear that many of Linden's users were there for the gambling, which was a reason for loss of users.

Another gating factor for many is the fact that you can only access Second Life from a machine with the software downloaded which restricts access and appeal. This is the same for other successful virtual worlds of commence, including Entropia and Utherverse, but it doesn't mean these worlds are irrelevant or should be ignored.

And there is real commerce taking place in virtual worlds which will increase over time, particularly as these worlds move into standard flash media such as the world of Webflock from the Electric Sheep company.

This means that those who laugh off Second Life's failure are wrong. Equally, those who think Second Life is dead and gone are wrong. I know of plenty of companies still using Second Life for virtual meetings and conferences, as well as other tools and universes.

Bottom line: don't discount virtual worlds quite yet, and there will be ways to make money out of these worlds through social finance as they mature.

The hype, 2007

> "In October 2006, Second Life (SL) had 1.2 million residents; in December 2007, they have 11.5 million."

The reality, January 2008

> "The actual number of SL users, those who logged in within the last 60 days, is just under 1.5 million, compared to March 2007 when SL had 4.458 million residents and 1.68 million users."

The reality, April 2009

> "The actual number of SL users, those who logged in within the last 60 days, is just under 1.5 million."

Talk to the bot (2008)

Yesterday was one of my 'futurism' days, where I spend time with bankers envisioning what the future of banking might look like.

We talked about all sorts of stuff, including chips inside people for payments and video banking ... some of my favourite themes. Then I got onto talking about avatars for a while. I guess you all know about avatars by now but, just in case, they are basically an electronic representation of you, usually in cartoon form.

This story illustrates it well.

The story is about British couple David Pollard and Amy Taylor, who met in an internet chatroom in 2004. They soon hooked up and fell in love with each other, as well as with the internet, and became avid users of the virtual world Second Life. Second Life allowed them to design and control virtual avatars of themselves that were really cool, so Amy became Laura Skye and David became Dave Barmby.

Their avatars are both good looking, slim people in their mid-20s, unlike Amy and David who, in real life, are rather large folks living on incapacity benefits. That's why you have a Second Life though, as it's meant to be better than your real life.

Anyways, they loved each other so much that they have a wedding in Second Life with all their virtual friends, as well as a wedding in real life.

Lovely.

Unfortunately, they end up not getting on so well a few years later, because Amy is now hooked on World of Warcraft. The virtual David is left to wander around Second Life all on his lonesome, as Laura Skye is off in the virtual woods, and Dave meets Modesty McDonnell, a 'hostess', who he engages in cybersex.

Just at that moment, Amy walks into the room in real life, to find a naked David sitting at his computer screen looking rather excited. Divorce ensues and Amy and David are no more. David is now with Linda Brinkley, a 55 year-old divorcee in Arkansas, US. Linda is the real world human behind the virtual hostess Modesty McDonnell, and David and Linda are engaged even though they have never met in real life. Meanwhile, Amy has run away with a priest in the World of Warcraft who she also met in her virtual life, and have now hooked up together in real life.

Moral of the story? Online dating: the odds are good, but the goods are odd.

Actually, the real moral is that more and more people are adjusting to lives that are dull in reality, but exciting and different online through avatars.

So I was talking about these ideas on the basis that, in a few years, we will all be designating the 'search' work of the internet to our avatars.

The virtual Chris will go to the bank of tomorrow, and interview them about their rates and deals. The virtual Chris will do this for all the credit cards and deposit accounts out there, and come back to recommend to me which are worth looking at. The result is that the real Chris no longer needs to search for financial services. I've delegated it to my automated avatar.

Now I can do this today, using websites such as Mint, but tomorrow my virtual avatar will do this by making comparison across all sites against my habits and needs. Equally, it will be comparing my financial habits and needs with all the other users of the internet, to make sure I get the deals most appropriate to my lifestyle. My avatar will do this so I don't' have to bother.

All well and good. It was at this point I had a realisation of a fundamental change in banking tomorrow.

If my avatar can go and find all this stuff on my behalf, then they could also switch my choice for me too. Therefore, rather than having my avatar recommend products to me, it could just switch me around between financial providers as better deals come up. In fact, switching could be done in real-time, regularly. Today, we think of 12-month contracts, six-month balance transfers, closing penalties and account opening overheads. Tomorrow, banks might deal with people jumping on and off ship in real time, with no penalties.

Think about it.

Today, I move my balance every five months and 28 days to ensure I never pay any interest on my credit card. Tomorrow, my avatar jumps around and does this for me fluidly non-stop.

Today, I change my mortgage every few years to lock in the most attractive fixed interest rate deal. Tomorrow, my avatar does this for me, non-stop, always moving to wherever they can optimise my savings versus borrowings.

The point of this is that if I have an intelligent avatar that can connect globally with other people's avatars and all of the financial service providers, and can also provide all the information and documentation required to open and close accounts, then what am I doing?

Sitting on the beach drinking a pina colada wondering why my avatar has lost all interest in cybersex and is talking about financial management all day long, of course.

Meanwhile, my bank is wondering how to ever get past my avatar's blocking techniques so that they can talk to me direct and offer some financial advice.

Go figure.

Virtual banking worlds become more realistic (2008)

For a while now, I have not posted a story about Second Life or other virtual worlds in banking ... because there has been no story to tell.

This is because the virtual bank collapses in Second Life during the summer of last year took the shine off this area a little. Although banks are still running internal operational meetings as avatars in there, as are other firms, there just has not been so much buzz about virtual worlds for a while.

Until now. Virtual worlds will be coming back with a vengeance, as Techcrunch report three new exciting developments.

The first is that the Electric Sheep Company, who design many of Second Life's commercial zones, has integrated virtual world capabilities into normal browser based systems. Called Webflock, the technology looks as good as Second Life, but it works using Flash media and ActiveX controls in a normal browser. No special downloads needed. I like the look and feel of this, and it is worth reading the Electric Sheep Company's blog, as they are the leaders in this field of future metaverses.

However, there's now competition as two other services are now available.

First there's Vivaty Scenes, a virtual world capability built into Facebook. Then there's the new Google service, Lively. Anything from Google is worth checking out, and this may prove to provide the killer app for virtual worlds' success as a browser-integrated service.

Between these three announcements, expect much more from Virtual Worlds in banking for the next year or two. This is because they are now available without having to download massive megabytes worth of applications to the desktop. In other words, virtual worlds are now fully enabled as web services.

That's the importance of these developments. Making virtual available anytime, anywhere, anyplace from any device.

Therefore, expect that the best virtual bank worlds to date will soon be available on a browser near you

Money laundering in virtual worlds (2007)

Now, we talk a lot about virtual worlds these days, after the hype cycle of Second Life and not forgetting the other worlds of Entropia, There, World of Warcraft and more. In fact, the growth of virtual worlds and MMORPGs (Massive Multiplayer Online Role Playing Games) has exploded over the past year and it is raising concerns in the risk community.

Maybe this is not surprising when a great deal of cash is flowing through such systems. For example, one nutter recently paid out over $10,000 for a virtual character in World of Warcraft according to Gizmodo: "The character, a rogue, came wielding the much prized Twin Blades of Azzinoth, which drop off big baddie Illidan Stormrage from the Black Temple."

Of course, we all know about this stuff don't we?

Even more notable is the cash flowing through Second Life, which is why it has had so much hype. Over one million real American crisp and shiny dollars are spent every day by the over 10 million residents in Second Life. Of these, there are over 400 residents who spend over Linden $1 million (around US$3,750) a month and around 100 transactions a month of over L$500,000 each (around $1,750).

The official view from the risk community is that it's not something that they are too concerned about right now, but they are watching. According to one friend in this community, they've now tracked seven distinct types of financial threat in the virtual economies. For example, Linden dollars are being used as a way to transact for services outside of Second Life anonymously. In other words, it's becoming an alternative electronic currency that can be traded and converted into real US dollars at will. This is specifically being used for pornography, where it allows complete anonymity at both ends of transactions for less than US$20.

Now, this may not worry us too much today, but the Chinese have been seriously worried by this development in their economy. This is because the population has caught onto the opportunities of using virtual currencies to avoid Big Brother big time.

In particular, China has a virtual currency called QQ which is part of Tencent QQ, China's largest instant messaging service provider's proposition. Tencent QQ has over 235 million users, and the QQ coin is worth the equivalent of 1 yuan (US$0.125).

Over 150 million people, many of them youngsters, buy QQ coins with yuan for downloads, cartoons, games, ringtones and other things for their mobile, avatar and blog. The thing is though, a bit like Second Life Linden dollar, the QQ became a popular currency to transact outside Tencent QQ for other gaming websites and, gradually, with call girls and gambling dens.

How does it work?

The basic operation is that a retailer sells QQ coins at a discount price. Customers pay for the QQ coins with Yuan through a debit card, money-order transfer or online payment service such as PayPal. The retailer then transfers the QQ coins to the buyer's account or gives the buyer access to the QQ account, where QQ coins are stored, by giving them their username and password.

According to one government estimate, the total volume of trading in virtual items in China last year was worth about $900 million. About 45% of that went for items in the Tencent QQ world. That's why the People's Republic of China started worrying, as almost a trillion dollars flowing through the economy going into illicit activities such as pornography and gambling is undesirable, to say the least.

So I would reckon that the risks of new worlds, new currencies, anonymous trading using prepaid and virtual accounts is going to create quite a challenge for risk managers in the future.

Deutsche Bank: refreshing innovations (2007)

I've been in a presentation from Deutsche Bank on Second Life. Actually, it was a presentation on how to emulate the bank experience in real life in Second Life, which is what Michael Tirpitz, Marketing Director, set out to achieve.

The first experiment however was how to innovate the real life experience in real life. This has been an ongoing prototyping and innovation project he´s been running in Berlin called Q110. Q110 is Quarter 110, as Berlin is divided into Quarter zones, and

Deutsche's branch on Felixstrasse has been transformed into a hub of innovation in branch store design.

From the street, the front of store looks like a retail shop. You look inside and yes, you can see banking products! That's because Deutsche have taken the traditional bank brochures describing their services and turned them into tangible tins and boxes. Inside the box you find a description of the product, plus a coupon for coffee and a gift. The coupon for coffee by the way, can be traded in-store to encourage you inside to meet the sales folks (what used to be called tellers!).

They've also partnered with Harrods, which has no stores in Germany, and offer Harrods-branded food ranges at the front of store. Food in a bank branch? You guessed it, this is no ordinary bank branch. In fact, from buying your banking tins with coupons for coffee to walking through the organic food hall at the front of store – you heard me – you get into the main guts of the branch and that's when you start finding mortgage, pensions, cashiers and so forth ... oh yes, and coffee, of course.

Then you ask me: where's the Second Life link, Chris?

Well, after rolling out the new innovations in Berlin last year, they've now copied the whole branch experience of Q110 and deployed this in Second Life in July 2007. This includes everything – even the branch staff! You go inside Deutsche's 110 zone online, and meet Olga who you know as the concierge in Felixstrasse. She guides you to the same designs and layout of advice, information and service as you see in Felixstrasse. You can even get your virtual coffee and drink it ... virtually, of course.

Unbelievable.

Mind you, the cash machine proves a bit more of a challenge as my PC printed Linden dollars rather than euros ... ah well, can't have everything.

BNP Paribas recruit staff in Second Life (2007)

Now most banks are getting in on the act of social networking and Second Life, with many opening branches; Saxo Bank opening a trading platform; and ING Direct opening a country: Our Virtual Holland. But now I find we have BNP Paribas using Second Life for a wholly different reason.

Recruitment.

If you're a budding developer and want a job with the bank, the first interview takes place between you and the banks' HR avatars. Prospective candidates begin by registering with the BNP Paribas website. Interviewees are then given an appointment in Second Life with details as to how to upload their avatar. The interview is then conducted between the HR avatar and the interviewee's.

What a great idea.

HR avatar: "What are your people skills like?"

Interviewee: "Well, my best friend is a character called Vixen Jane in Pratts Bottom."

HR avatar: "... next!"

Why Wells Fargo left Second Life (2007)

Tim Collins' presentation on "Joining Online Communities: Marketing in New Environments" at the Financial Services Club last night was interesting. Tim is the Senior Vice President for Experiential Marketing at Wells Fargo, and I invited him to talk to the Financial Services Club about virtual worlds, corporate blogging and related matters.

The main subject that attracted interest was Wells Fargo's use of Second Life, as it was the first bank to be in there using this virtual world for connecting with its targeted student community. The trial began in September 2005 with a pilot designed to deliver a financial education message in a fun, engaging way. Further to this trial, Wells Fargo committed to taking these virtual world services to a higher level and moved the experiment to its own platform, Stagecoach Island.

It was of particular interest to me to understand the reasoning for Wells Fargo leaving Second Life and creating its own separate platform. Tim explained that this was due to a number of factors including the fact that this gave them:

- Increased flexibility;
- Increased consumer availability;
- A better brand fit;
- Lower cost;
- Increased activities, such as Sunday brunches, skydiving clubs and so on; and
- The provision of additional financial education content.

All sounds well and good, although you may wonder about some of the items above so here's an explanation of increasing activities.

Wells Fargo would arrange social activities, such as everyone getting together for flying lessons – the sort of stuff people do in Second Life – and said that, at the time, if more than 20 people turned up the system slowed down and if over 40 came along then the system would come to a dead stop.

Another more subtle reason for Wells Fargo coming out of Second Life came out of the discussion that followed when Tim played a video of an interview with Ailin Graef. She's the girl who made over a $1 million – real US dollars – out of land that doesn't exist.

She did this by buying and selling virtual land and properties in Second Life using Linden dollars, with around 266 Linden dollars to a US dollar at current exchange rates. Through her ability to buy early on in Second Life's developments, she's made a fortune by selling hot properties in the main downtown strips of this other world.

The video Tim played was of an interview in Second Life with her on CNET.com news, who decided to interview Ailin's her online avatar, a character called Anshe Chung. The interview was going to be all about her success and how she had achieved such riches. However, before the interview could start, angry Second Life network terrorists bombed the interview by sending a flock of flying ... urrmmm ... male genitalia (in cartoon form) into the CNET news room.

For this reason, Wells Fargo determined it would be better to launch its own platform, powered by Second Life, as it would have more control over what content went out.

So, it's all well and good to use social networks when the form of community is the written word, but when you move to images and live cartoon dialogues, then be careful ... it could just give you the willies.

Beware the hype curve (2007)

Last week's announcements by ING of the launch of a Virtual Holland in Second Life, following hard on the heels of ABN AMRO's branch in there, was covered widely by other blogs and chats on Finextra.

This is the stuff of gimmicks though, as I've been watching Second Life and originally one in every two users regularly visited the site, now it's more like one in three. This is down to the hype curve – where people go and look once and then never again.

For example, Second Life shows the number of regular visitors versus residents (registrations) on the home page. Over the last six months, the registrations have quadrupled, while the real users have tripled. Here are a few statistics to substantiate:

	Logged in Last 60 days	Residents (registered users)	US$ spent last 24 hours
October 2006	500,000	1.2 million	$500k
January 2007	1.1 million	3.5 million	$1.3 million
March 2007	1.55 million	4.4 million	$1.5 million

So, the trend is that real users are growing fast, but not as fast as the hype, whilst the level of spend seems fairly consistent at $1 per day per user, near enough. Therefore, with a bankroll doubling every quarter based upon current trends it's worth being in there, and that is why banks are opening branches and islands in Second Life.

In particular, the Dutch are known to be innovators and so it does not surprise me that ING and ABN AMRO are some of the first to be in there, although it should be noted that Wells Fargo's Stagecoach Island has been around longer and is the one I'm watching, especially as there's now over 100 Stagecoach Island virtual millionaires.

And this is what the banks are after - the social networking, Web 2.0 bankroll. Is it in Second Life? No.

Don't get me wrong. I'm a total believer in the social networking trend – MySpace, YouTube etc – and what banks can get out of it, so this is all interesting stuff. However, it is Zopa and Prosper that will be the really viable versions of next generation banking, whilst Second Life is just another version of There.com, which has been around since 2002 and I've been a member for four years. There, Second Life, World of Warcraft, Everquest – they're all just online interactive cartoons. All of them are transient worlds that every now and again catch the media's, and therefore the public's eye. But then it moves on. Give it another year and the new massively multiplayer online game from Lego will probably have taken over.

Should ING, ABN AMRO and Wells Fargo create branches and operations in all of these worlds or will they just go for the one's that happen to have the media coverage?

No comment. But with today's Lego game announcement, I'd open a branch in there. After all, it's all about clicks and bricks ...

Chapter 6 Social media in practice

The
Complete
Banker

Introduction

It's still early days for banks to put social media into practice. There are a few, however. For example, Wells Fargo's Stagecoach Island and Barclays Bank's 56 Sage Street. In both examples, the idea is to have fun in virtual worlds whilst learning the disciplines of financial management. TD in Canada have a group of over 20,000 fans on Facebook in their Money Lounge, with a specific area for students. One of my favourite bank services is *Tu Cuentas* from BBVA in Spain, where they offer an iPhone and Android-based banking service that brings in all the best things on the internet, such as budgeting apps that compare your financial behaviours with all the other BBVA customers to advise and help you get the best out of the bank. There are a few other worthwhile examples out there, with the common element in all of these mobile and internet services is that they are trying to make banking fun and interesting, rather than boring and staid. In other words, to socialise banking.

Wells Fargo: a lesson in Web 2.0 (2008)

I was delighted to host Wells Fargo at the Financial Services Club last night. Wells gave an update on their Web 2.0 strategies, which are far and away ahead of most other banks in Europe. This was corroborated by the bankers attending, who said to me afterwards that they were stunned by just how leading edge some of Wells Fargo's online distribution services are, compared to their own.

For example, if we start with basic blogging, Wells Fargo has been blogging for a few years now. They began with *Guided by History,* and now have the Student Loandown, Commercial Electronic Office and Stagecoach Island blogs. Each is designed for a different audience, and covers all aspects of the history and breadth of the bank.

The bank's view is that if you're invited to the party and don't attend, then people are going to trash you, and that's exactly what happened to Wells Fargo a few years ago. They weren't on the internet, and some joker started posting horror stories about bad service at the bank. That joker's stories became a website called Wells Fargo Sucks, and was coming top of the listings when you searched for Wells Fargo on Google. However, by blogging and actively deploying online media strategies, this site has now slipped well down the google listings. For example, Google 'Wells Fargo' today, and it doesn't even appear in the first few pages of results.

In other words, by leveraging the internet by writing and socialising about the bank online, you can change the profile of the bank on the internet. And this was the learning lesson from last night. By being at the party and engaging with the folks online, you get into a conversation and it is far more civilised and interactive than leaving folks to talk about you without a response.

As a result, the bank went a step further and focused upon other online services such as Facebook and YouTube.

YouTube had lots of videos of people who talked about the bank in a dismissive way. What do you do about that? Answer: launch a competition to create the best version of the Wells Fargo song from the musical, 'The Music Man'. Wells Fargo launched the competition a year ago, and aired the winning video as a prime-time advert during the College Football final at the Rose Bowl, watched by over 40 million American viewers. The side effect was that the videos made as entries flooded YouTube, and hence drowned out some of the negative videos posted there with positive viewings.

Similarly, in another strand of intelligent online marketing, they have recently started a series about 'Someday Stories'. These are stories of folks who have a dream and the five finalists have been selected. The finalists win $10,000 each and every story is quite emotional. For example, about illness, the loss of a loved one or something similar. Now, Wells Fargo's customers can vote for the most worthy story and that winner gets $100,000 prize.

It's a reality show for the internet age in other words, and the stories again form videos for YouTube and advertising. It also extends to Facebook and other online networks. It even gets talked about in other websites favourably, such as the Fashionable Housewife.

In totality, what this tells me is that Wells Fargo, based in California and at the heart of the internet age, understands online marketing for banking today.

One of the few.

Wells Fargo + Wachovia = The Merger Blog (2009)

Wells Fargo has gained a lot of coverage from the blogging community about their own launch of a blog.

This one explains the details involved in the Wells Fargo/ Wachovia merger to the world at large, with the first entry from Wells' President and CEO John Stumpf.

John says they needed to launch the blog because: "Blending cultures, combining businesses, products and systems, and changing names will take time – two to three years – because we want to do it right for you."

As mentioned, lots of bloggers are blogging about the blog itself (now there's a tongue twister).

Colin Henderson at The Bankwatch reports that this "is the first example of a large company to use social media to help with a major merger and product integration of this size."

Forrester's Jermiah Owyang says that: "While most corporate blogs aren't trusted, it's refreshing to see a new type of blog appear to meet the needs of transparency, no n-pitching, and openness with the community – yet meet the business needs of the corporations."

Whilst Paul Penrose at Finextra disagrees: "Don't expect a warts-and-all free-for-all. Another of the site's lead bloggers is Matt Wadley, a member of Wachovia's corporate communications department. Matt promises that the blog won't just be another channel for corporate PR. All the same, the information spun through this channel is likely to be tightly controlled. If the three-year integration project starts running into problems don't expect to hear it here first."

There are more.

My own view? This is a long-term blog, two to three years as John Stumpf states. Therefore, this could prove interesting in creating a corporate case study in how to manage a merger ... or how not to. I doubt it's the latter though as, with over 100 mergers successfully completed under Mr. Stumpf's belt, this one should work.

Result? Harvard and other business schools will watch this merger and this blog very carefully to see what transpires, as will I.

Wells tell me already that the blog is off to a good start. After less than a day, they are already on the first page of Google, when you search for Wells Fargo Wachovia, and that's the first page from over 2.2 million sites. Equally, the site garnered 50 consumer comments overnight, which is more than all of Wells Fargo's other blogs combined.

Equally, as I've reported before, Wells are good with social media. You've even got these guys on Twitter.

Therefore, I'm interested to see how this transpires as most banks don't even do any blogging or twittering. For example, where's the HBOS/Lloyds TSB blog, JPMorgan/Washington Mutual blog, Bank of America/Merrill Lynch blog ...

(Stagecoach) Islands in the Stream (2009)

I've blogged a lot about Wells Fargo's innovations in the past.

This is because they are one of the banks in the stream of innovation that comes out of Silicon Valley. This is why they are great proponents of social media:

- Blogging: FIVE corporate blogs;
- Online video: YouTube channel;
- Social networks: MySpace profile for Cassie, from Stagecoach Island;
- Facebook Stagecoach Island application and fan page;
- Virtual worlds: Stagecoach Island.

Stagecoach Island is one of their key platforms in this space. It was first piloted in September 2005 to provide financial education in a fun and engaging way.

Initially, it was piloted in Second Life but, after some issues over virtual hackers and bombers, Wells Fargo moved Stagecoach Island onto their own platform in 2006.

Three years later, it is still going, with its own community, blog and Facebook fanbase.

So I was intrigued yesterday when I saw that they've just launched the Stagecoach Island University (the official launch was on November 30th).

What's this, I wondered? And so I asked Tim Collins, who looks after experiential marketing at Wells Fargo, to tell all. I also gave him a hard time over some of the sceptics' views on the value of these developments.

Here's our chat:

Tim: We continue to be happy with the results of Stagecoach Island and invest in new features every year. We have tens of thousands of members and see double digit growth in membership every year. Engagement is also growing, as our session lengths are approaching an hour.

We are about to launch Stagecoach Island University, which was created in partnership with Educational Financial Services and WF Foundation. The 'Admissions' module expands the Stagecoach Island curriculum to include saving for college, financial aid, tips for budgeting and information on funding post secondary education. The 'University' content provides direct access to the entire young adult and adult sections of Hands-on Banking in a virtual space.

To add a user incentive component and incorporate real world lessons, once members complete their university experience and pass a comprehensive exit exam, they will be eligible for a new tier of 'high-level' jobs within Stagecoach Island, each of which requires the completion of Stagecoach Island University.

Chris: In other words, by completing the Stagecoach Island University examinations, users become more knowledgeable about their finances and use of money, and should be better capable of managing budgets, borrowings and investments.

Tim: That's right.

Chris: But the sceptics out there always ask me the same questions about this stuff.

Tim: Such as?

Chris: Well, the first question would be: why would a bank keep investing in virtual worlds as most virtual world experiments, such as all the banking trials in Second Life, are dead and gone. Isn't this a broken business model?

Tim: I don't think it's fair to compare Stagecoach Island to Second Life. It's like comparing a private community to the entire blogosphere. Stagecoach Island is a private community with an educational purpose. Second Life has a generalist business model in a world that is increasingly specialized. They are adapting, but since their data security breach, I doubt many financial services companies will want to engage with them.

Chris: OK, even if this is worth doing, aren't all the users young, zero profit students, or are there any real people on Stagecoach Island?

Tim: Our average age for a user is 23 years old, but we have learned that our members are much more profitable than your average 23 year old. They have higher balances, more products, and will recommend us to their friends. And did I mention their great dental hygiene? :-)

Chris: Can you provide any proof points that show this to be a worthwhile venture?

Tim: I think I just did.

Chris: Maybe, but every time I mention what you're doing to others, those are the questions I get.

Tim: I'm not surprised. Bankers are a literal audience. They want to see a direct cause and effect. If they spend a dollar on marketing today, how much will I get in sales and profits tomorrow? Experiential marketing is different. It doesn't directly support the sales process. Rather, it's the warm-up act for the sales process. If we invest the time and effort to educate consumers, whether they be our customers or not, they will think kindly of us when it comes time to doing their banking. It will make the sales process easier, and we will make more money. We have proved this with project after project ... social media as a prime example. I think you are getting these questions because many companies don't have the patience.

Chris: Thanks Tim, and good luck with it all.

First Direct leading the social finance mainstream (2009)

For over four years, since Facebook first appeared on my radar, I've been waiting for a UK bank to really get into social media. There have been a few attempts but nothing really mainstream. For example, the Co-operative launched a MySpace site for Good with Money and Barclaycard did some good things, but most was a gimmick or poorly delivered.

Generally, however, UK banks are reticent when it comes to blogs, podcasts, interaction and Web 2.0. Finally, for the first time, one gets it.

First Direct. First Direct launched its social media newsroom in June this year ... and it has been on Twitter since April 27th ... and has 464 followers and 168 tweets as of today.

So it's great to see it launch a truly open dialogue in their Live area, which was announced in the newsroom yesterday.

> "We wanted to give our customers the opportunity to talk back and let us know how they really feel about us. With this in mind we recently launched our new acquisition campaign – 'Live'. It works by taking everything that's said about us online, from over 8 million forums, blogs and social media sites, and then feeding it, live, onto our website www.firstdirect.com/live for all to see. At the same time we also launched Talking Point - a section where customers can leave a message for us."

Viewing the Live home page, you get some nice commentary to encourage you to dialogue, and it clearly highlights some of the positive views as well as the negative. In fact they clearly demonstrate how positive or negative customers are being overall with + signs for positive and - for negative floating up and down the home page, in real time we assume ...

So hats off to First Direct for being at the forefront of UK financial social media. In fact, a real hats off as you can find all of this easily from its home page, as, being Mr. Cynical, some would think this would be hidden away in some microsite somewhere.

Only a bank voted consistently number one by independent surveys would have such confidence to do this, of course.

And, just as a reality check, I thought I should see if any other UK bank had a blog, twitter link or anything on their home page to demonstrate social interactivity.

Lloyds TSB? Nope. No blog or anything.

NatWest? Nope. No podcasts or anything there on the home page.

Barclays Bank seemed to be better as, on their homepage they have a clear area prompting customers to ask a question, so I thought I would search for where's their blog? 'Can't find the answer? Contact us.'

UK banks generally don't offer anything social on their internet presence today: no Facebook, Twitter, blog, podcast or even interactive live chat. It does confirm that banks don't want to interact with customers online ... only on the telephone or in branch.

At least First Direct is demonstrating some leadership here and it will be interesting to see how its service develops as the first UK bank to be in the forefront of this space ... a bit like it was the first UK bank to lead the telephone banking revolution.

Update from First Direct's CEO on their social experiment (2009)

Matt Colebrook, First Direct's Chief Executive, has just written his initial observations about their social media experiment. Interesting words:

"It's now over four weeks since we launched our pioneering 'Live' site and we've been overwhelmed with how it's been received, over 2000 comments to date on a wide variety of topics.

"We've also seen a huge amount of positive comments about the site in the press, online and in social media. People have described it as brave. They might be right. What's undeniable is that it's been the right thing to do if we're to engage with our customers and understand how they feel towards us.

"We're starting to analyse the thoughts, concerns and suggestions raised with a view to seeing where we might make improvements to the service and offerings we already provide. Clearly we can't be all things to all people.

"Indeed we won't be able to offer everything that has been suggested. But one thing we can and will do is at least capture and digest what our customers are saying. We are also introducing a way for us to join in the conversations on 'live' and I will soon start to feed back more detailed responses to some of the comments being left.

"The world of social media is one that is opening up a new voice for customers – we might not always get it right but you can be assured that happy customers are at the heart of our business. It's what differentiates us from our competitors."

Banco Sabadell – the iPad bank (2010)

It surprises me how often I find Spanish banks surprise me. First, BBVA launch the first really cool bank 2.0 apps two years ago. Then Caja Navarra launches a fantastic hybrid Zopa-Bank-styled

P2P lending service. More recently, Santander created a really interesting head office campus full of robots.

And now Banco Sabadell is one of the first, if not the first bank to launch an iPad banking service.

My good friend Pol Navarro, Director for Innovation at Banco Sabadell, tells me that they decided to do this because: "Since we launched our mobile portal, at the end of 2009, we've seen a tremendous usage from iPhone users – about 60% of access – so we decided to develop a specific app for the iPhone/iPad."

Certainly, that seems to be indicative of a core focus upon the customer as, in just three months since its launch, Banco Sabadell's Mobile Service (BSMS) is being used by more than 13,500 customers of the bank and is expected to exceed their target of 35,000 customers this year.

According to the bank's blog – yes, they have a blog! – the "new version of BS Mobile for iPhone IPAD includes all operations currently available in the BS Mobile service (consulting accounts and cards, transfers and transfers, purchase / sale of securities, signature files, etc. ..) for both the segment private customers and companies, taking advantage of new capabilities for interaction and usability that Apple devices offer and improving current features:

Tracking all current procedures of the customer (card applications, loans, etc ...) to give the best customer service and information wherever you are.

- Higher quality maps and greater precision in the location of offices and ATMs, as well as Street View;
- New presentation of the application, Touch and more intuitive;
- Ability to save favourite operations and menu customization operations;
- Keyboard shortcuts to the operations of accounts, cards, data transfers and your personal manager;

- Option to call me back for easy access to the Contact Center."

In addition, Pol tells me that they "think that the iPad has its own space, for consuming digital content online/offline (airplanes, garden, home, etc.) ... the iPad version, has some specific functions, adapted to the terminal's screen size, user interaction, maps navigation, etc."

They are also developing the iPad further: "For example, product simulation of loans and mortgages, investment portfolios, video calls with your sales rep, etc. Also this kind of gadget can be used internally, for sales rep, private banking advisors, etc. We are just investigating in this side."

All in all, Spanish banks never fail to impress me with their first mover experiments in social and mobile finance. Definitely not a case of mañana, my friend.

www.ingramcontent.com/pod-product-compliance
Ingram Content Group UK Ltd.
Pitfield, Milton Keynes, MK11 3LW, UK
UKHW041824200726
13854UKWH00002BA/553